The Reawakening

The Reawakening

(La Tregua)

A LIBERATED PRISONER'S LONG MARCH HOME
THROUGH EAST EUROPE

by

PRIMO LEVI

Translated from the Italian by
STUART WOOLF

An Atlantic Monthly Press Book
LITTLE, BROWN AND COMPANY · BOSTON · TORONTO

LIBRARY OF CONGRESS CATALOG CARD NO. 65–10907

FIRST AMERICAN EDITION

Published in England under the title THE TRUCE.

ATLANTIC–LITTLE, BROWN BOOKS
ARE PUBLISHED BY
LITTLE, BROWN AND COMPANY
IN ASSOCIATION WITH
THE ATLANTIC MONTHLY PRESS

Published simultaneously in Canada
by Little, Brown & Company (Canada) Limited

PRINTED IN THE UNITED STATES OF AMERICA

CONTENTS

Dreams used to come in the brutal nights,
Dreams crowding and violent
Dreamt with body and soul,
Of going home, of eating, of telling our story.
Until, quickly and quietly, came
The dawn reveille:
            Wstawàch.
And the heart cracked in the breast.

Now we have found our home again,
Our hunger is quenched,
All the stories have been told.
It is time. Soon we shall hear again
The alien command:
            Wstawàch.

11 January, 1946

The author's route home

LEO VERNON

The Reawakening

1. The Thaw

IN THE FIRST days of January 1945, hard pressed by the Red Army, the Germans hastily evacuated the Silesian mining region. But whereas elsewhere, in analogous conditions, they had not hesitated to destroy the Lagers and their inhabitants by fire or arms, they acted differently in the district of Auschwitz: superior orders had been received (given personally, it would seem, by Hitler) to recover at all costs every man fit for work. Thus all healthy prisoners were evacuated, in frightful conditions, in the direction of Buchenwald and Mauthausen, while the sick were abandoned to their fate. One can legitimately deduce from the evidence that originally the Germans did not intend to leave even one man alive in the concentration camps; but a fierce night air raid and the rapidity of the Russian advance induced them to change their minds and flee, leaving their task unfinished.

In the sick bay of the Lager at Buna-Monowitz eight hundred of us remained. Of these about five hundred died from illness, cold and hunger before the Russians arrived, and another two hundred succumbed in the following days, despite the Russians' aid.

The first Russian patrol came in sight of the camp about midday on 27th January 1945. Charles and I were the first to see them: we were carrying Sómogyi's body to the common grave, the first of our room mates to die. We tipped the stretcher on to the defiled snow, as the pit was now full, and no other grave was at hand: Charles took off his beret as a salute to both the living and the dead.

They were four young soldiers on horseback, who advanced along the road that marked the limits of the camp, cautiously holding their sten-guns. When they reached the barbed wire, they stopped to look, exchanging a few timid words, and throwing strangely embarrassed glances at the sprawling bodies, at the battered huts, and at us few still alive.

To us they seemed wonderfully concrete and real, perched on their enormous horses, between the grey of the snow and the grey of the sky, immobile beneath the gusts of damp wind which threatened a thaw.

It seemed to us, and so it was, that the nothing full of death in which we had wandered like spent stars for ten days had found its own solid centre, a nucleus of condensation; four men, armed, but not against us: four messengers of peace, with rough and boyish faces beneath their heavy fur hats.

They did not greet us, nor did they smile; they seemed oppressed not only by compassion but by a confused restraint, which sealed their lips and bound their eyes to the funereal scene. It was that shame we knew so well, the shame that drowned us after the selections, and every time we had to watch, or submit to, some outrage: the shame the Germans did not know, that the just man experiences at another man's crime; the feeling of guilt that such a crime should exist, that it should have been introduced irrevocably into the world of things that exist, and that his will for good should have proved too weak or null, and should not have availed in defence.

So for us even the hour of liberty rang out grave and muffled, and filled our souls with joy and yet with a painful sense of pudency, so that we should have liked to wash our consciences and our memories clean from the foulness that lay upon them; and also with anguish, because we felt that this should never happen, that now nothing could ever happen good and pure enough to rub out our past, and that the scars of the outrage would remain within us for ever, and in the memories of those who saw it, and in the places where it

Lager of Auschwitz, now transformed into a gigantic lazaret.

In the meantime, the thaw we had been fearing for so many days had started, and as the snow slowly disappeared, the camp began to change into a squalid bog. The bodies and the filth made the misty, muggy air impossible to breathe. Nor had death ceased to take its toll: the sick died in their cold bunks by the dozen, and here and there along the muddy roads, as if suddenly struck down, died the greediest of the survivors, those who had followed blindly the imperious command of our age-old hunger and had stuffed themselves with the rations of meat that the Russians, still engaged in fighting, sent irregularly to the camp: sometimes little, sometimes nothing, sometimes in crazy abundance.

But I was aware of what was going on around me in only a disconnected and hazy manner. It seemed as if the weariness and the illness, like ferocious and cowardly beasts, had waited in ambush for the moment when I dismantled my defences, in order to attack me from behind. I lay in a feverish torpor, semi-conscious, tended fraternally by Charles, and tormented by thirst and acute pains in my joints. There were no doctors or drugs. I also had a sore throat, and half my face had swollen; my skin had become red and rough and hurt me like a burn; perhaps I was suffering from more than one illness at the same time. When it was my turn to climb on to Yankel's cart, I was no longer able to stand on my feet.

I was hoisted on to the cart by Charles and Arthur, together with a load of dying men, from whom I did not feel very different. It was drizzling, and the sky was low and gloomy. While the slow steps of Yankel's horses drew me towards remote liberty, for the last time there filed before my eyes the huts where I had suffered and matured, the Roll-call square where the gallows and the gigantic Christmas tree still towered side by side, and the gate to slavery, on which one could still read the three, now hollow, words of derision: '*Arbeit Macht Frei*', 'Work Gives Freedom'.

2. The Main Camp

AT BUNA WE did not know much of 'the main camp', of Auschwitz proper: the Häftlinge transferred from one camp to another were few, hardly talkative (no Häftling ever was), and not easily believed.

When Yankel's cart crossed the famous threshold, we were amazed. Buna-Monowitz, with its twelve thousand inhabitants, was a village in comparison: what we were entering now was a boundless metropolis. There were no one-storey 'Blocks', but innumerable gloomy, square, grey stone edifices, three floors high, all identical; between them ran paved roads, straight and at right angles, as far as the eye could see. Everything was deserted, silent, flattened by the heavy sky, full of mud and rain and abandonment.

Here too, as at every turn of our long itinerary, we were surprised to be greeted with a bath, when we had need of so many other things. But this was no bath of humiliation, no grotesque-devilish-sacral bath, no black-mass bath like the first one which had marked our descent into the concentration-camp universe, nor was it a functional, antiseptic, highly automatized bath, like that of our passage into American hands many months later: it was a bath in the Russian manner, to human measure, extemporaneous and crude.

I am not questioning that a bath was opportune for us in our condition: in fact it was necessary, and not unwelcome. But in that bath, and at each of those three memorable christenings, it was easy to perceive behind the concrete and literal aspect a great symbolic shadow, the unconscious desire of the new authorities, who absorbed us in turn within their own sphere, to strip us of the vestiges of our former life, to make of us new men consistent with their own models, to impose their brand upon us.

The robust arms of two Soviet nurses lifted us down from the cart: '*Po malu!*' ('gently, gently!'); these were the first Russian words I heard. They were two energetic and experienced girls. They led us to one of the installations of the Lager, which had been summarily restored, undressed us, made us lie down on the wooden laths that covered the floor, and with tender hands, but without too much regard, soaped, rubbed, massaged and dried us from head to foot.

The operation went smoothly and quickly for all of us, except for some moralistic-jacobin protests from Arthur, who proclaimed himself *libre citoyen*, and in whose subconscious the contact of those feminine hands upon his bare skin conflicted with ancestral taboos. But a serious obstacle intervened when it came to the turn of the last of our group.

None of us knew who he was, because he was in no condition to speak. He was a shadow, a bald little figure, twisted like a root, skeleton-like, knotted up by a horrible contraction of all his muscles; they had lifted him out of the cart bodily, like an inanimate block, and now he lay on the ground on his side, curled up and stiff, in a desperate position of defence, with his knees pressed up against his forehead, his elbows squeezed against his sides, and his hands like wedges, with the fingers pressing against his shoulders. The Russian sisters, perplèxed, sought in vain to stretch him on his back, at which he let out shrill mouse-like squeaks: it was in any case a useless effort; his limbs yielded elastically under pressure, but as soon as they were released, they shot back to their initial position. Then the nurses came to a decision and carried him under the shower as he was; and because they had definite orders, they washed him as best they could, forcing the sponge and soap into the entangled knots of his body; finally, they rinsed him conscientiously, throwing a couple of buckets of tepid water over him.

Charles and I, naked and steaming, watched the scene with compassion and horror. When one of the arms was stretched out, we saw the tattooed number for a moment: he was a 200,000, one from the Vosges: *'Bon dieu, c'est un français!'* exclaimed Charles, and turned in silence towards the wall.

We were given a shirt and pants, and led to the Russian barber, so that our heads might be shaved for the last time in our careers. The barber was a dark-skinned giant, with wild and delirious eyes: he practised his art with uncouth violence, and for reasons unknown to me carried a sten-gun slung on his shoulder. *'Italiano Mussolini'*, he said to me grimly; and to the two Frenchmen *'Fransé Laval'*; from which one sees how little general ideas help the understanding of individual cases.

Here we split up: Charles and Arthur, cured and relatively healthy, rejoined the French group and disappeared from my horizon. I, being ill, was taken to the infirmary, given a summary medical check, and urgently relegated to a new 'Infectious Ward'.

The infirmary was such both by design, and also because it was indeed overflowing with invalids (in fact the Germans in flight had left only the most seriously ill at Monowitz, Auschwitz, and Birkenau, and these had all been collected together by the Russians in the Main Camp); it was not, nor could it be, a place for treatment, because the doctors (mostly ill themselves) numbered only a few dozen, drugs and sanitary equipment were wholly lacking, while at least three-quarters of the five thousand camp-inmates were in need of treatment.

The place to which I was consigned was a huge and gloomy dormitory, filled to the ceiling with suffering and moaning. For perhaps eight hundred patients there was only one doctor on duty and no nurse: the patients had themselves to provide for their most urgent needs, and for those of their sicker companions. I spent only one night there, which I still remember as a nightmare; in the morning the corpses in the bunks or sprawling on the floor could be counted by the dozen.

The following day I was transferred to a smaller ward with only twenty bunks; I lay in one of these for three or four days, prostrated by a high fever, conscious only intermittently, incapable of eating, and tormented by thirst.

On the fifth day the fever had disappeared. I felt as light as a cloud, famished and frozen, but my head was clear, my eyes and ears felt as if purified by the enforced vacation, and I was able to re-establish contact with the world.

In the course of those few days a striking change had occurred around me. It was the last great sweep of the scythe, the closing of accounts; the dying were dead, in all the others life was beginning to flow again tumultuously. Outside the windows, despite the steady snowfall, the mournful roads of the camp were no longer deserted, but teemed with a brisk, confused and noisy ferment, which seemed to be an end in itself. Cheerful or wrathful calls, shouts and songs rang out till late at night. All the same, my attention, and that of my neighbours in the nearby beds, rarely managed to escape from the obsessive presence, the mortal power of affirmation of the smallest and most harmless among us, of the most innocent, of a child, of Hurbinek.

Hurbinek was a nobody, a child of death, a child of Auschwitz. He looked about three years old, no one knew anything of him, he could not speak and he had no name; that curious name, Hurbinek, had been given to him by us, perhaps by one of the women who had interpreted with those syllables one of the inarticulate sounds that the baby let out now and again. He was paralysed from the waist down, with atrophied legs, as thin as sticks; but his eyes, lost in his triangular and wasted face, flashed terribly alive, full of demand, assertion, of the will to break loose, to shatter the tomb of his dumbness.

21

The speech he lacked, which no one had bothered to teach him, the need of speech charged his stare with explosive urgency: it was a stare both savage and human, even mature, a judgement, which none of us could support, so heavy was it with force and anguish.

None of us, that is, except Henek; he was in the bunk next to me, a robust and hearty Hungarian boy of fifteen. Henek spent half his day beside Hurbinek's pallet. He was maternal rather than paternal; had our precarious coexistence lasted more than a month, it is extremely probable that Hurbinek would have learnt to speak from Henek; certainly better than from the Polish girls who, too tender and too vain, inebriated him with caresses and kisses, but shunned intimacy with him.

Henek, on the other hand, calm and stubborn, sat beside the little sphinx, immune to the distressing power he emanated; he brought him food to eat, adjusted his blankets, cleaned him with skilful hands, without repugnance; and he spoke to him, in Hungarian naturally, in a slow and patient voice. After a week, Henek announced seriously, but without a shadow of selfconsciousness, that Hurbinek 'could say a word'. What word? He did not know, a difficult word, not Hungarian: something like 'mass-klo', 'matisklo'. During the night we listened carefully: it was true, from Hurbinek's corner there occasionally came a sound, a word. It was not, admittedly, always exactly the same word, but it was certainly an articulated word; or better, several slightly different articulated words, experimental variations on a theme, on a root, perhaps on a name.

Hurbinek continued in his stubborn experiments for as long as he lived. In the following days everybody listened to him in silence, anxious to understand, and among us there were speakers of all the languages of Europe; but Hurbinek's word remained secret. No, it was certainly not a message, it was not a revelation; perhaps it was his name, if it had ever fallen to his lot to be given a name; perhaps (according to one of our hypotheses) it meant 'to eat' or, 'bread'; or perhaps 'meat' in Bohemian, as one of us who knew that language maintained.

Hurbinek, who was three years old and perhaps had been born in Auschwitz and had never seen a tree; Hurbinek, who had fought like a man, to the last breath, to gain his entry into the world of men, from which a bestial power had excluded him; Hurbinek, the nameless, whose tiny forearm – even his – bore the tattoo of Auschwitz; Hurbinek died in the first days of March 1945, free but not redeemed. Nothing remains of him: he bears witness through these words of mine.

Henek was a good companion, and a perpetual source of surprise. His name too, like that of Hurbinek, was artificial: his real name, which was König, had been changed into Henek, a Polish diminutive for Henry, by the two Polish girls who, although at least ten years older than him, felt for Henek an ambiguous sympathy which soon turned into open desire.

Henek-König, alone of our microcosm of affliction, was neither ill nor convalescent; in fact he enjoyed splendid physical and spiritual health. He was of small stature and mild aspect, but he had the muscles of an athlete; he was affectionate and obliging towards Hurbinek and us, yet harboured sedate, sanguinary instincts. The Lager, a mortal trap, a 'bone-crusher' for the others, had been a good school for him; in a few months it had made of him a young carnivore, alert, shrewd, ferocious and prudent.

In the long hours we passed together he told me the chief events of his short life. He was born and lived on a farm in the middle of a wood in Transylvania, near the Rumanian border. On Sundays, he and his father often went to the woods, both with guns. Why with guns? To hunt? Yes, to hunt; but also to shoot at Rumanians. And why shoot at Rumanians? Because they are Rumanians, Henek explained to me with disarming simplicity. Every now and again they also shot at us.

He had been captured and deported to Auschwitz with his whole family. The others had been killed at once; he had told the S.S. that he was eighteen years old and a bricklayer, when he was really only fourteen and a schoolboy. So he entered Birkenau; but at Birkenau he had insisted on his real age, had been assigned to the children's Block, and, as he was the oldest and most robust, had become their Kapo. The children at Birkenau were like birds of passage: after a few days they were transferred to the Experiments Block, or directly to the gas chambers. Henek had understood the situation immediately, and like a good Kapo he had 'organized' himself, he had established solid relations with an influential Hungarian Häftling, and had remained until the liberation. When there were selections at the children's Block he was the one who chose. Did he feel no remorse? No: why should he? Was there any other way to survive?

At the evacuation of the Lager, he had wisely decided to hide; from his hiding-place, through the small window of a cellar, he had seen the Germans empty the fabulous storehouses of Auschwitz in great haste, and he had noted that in the hurry of their departure, they had scattered a fair number of tins of food on the road. They had not stopped to recover them, but had sought to destroy them by driving their half-tracks over them. Many tins had been driven into the mud and snow without splitting open; at night Henek had come out with a sack and had collected a fantastic hoard of tins, deformed, flattened, but still full: meat, lard, fish, fruit, vitamins. Naturally he had not said anything to anybody: he told me about it, because I was in the neighbouring bunk, and because I could be of use to him in guarding them. In fact, as Henek spent many hours wandering around the Lager on mysterious errands, while I was incapable of moving, my work as custodian was quite useful to him. He had faith in me; he settled the sack under my bed, and during the following days recompensed me with a fair wage in kind, authorizing me to take such extra rations as he judged proportionate to my services and suitable, in quality and quantity, to my condition as an invalid.

Hurbinek was not the only child. There were others, in relatively good health; they had formed a little 'club', very closed and reserved, in which the intrusion of adults was visibly unwelcome. They were wild and judicious little animals, who conversed in languages I could not understand. The most authoritative member of the clan was no more than five years old, and his name was Peter Pavel.

Peter Pavel spoke to nobody and had need of nobody. He was a beautiful blond and robust child, with an intelligent and impassive face. In the morning he climbed down from his bunk, which was on the third tier, with slow but sure movements, went to the showers to fill his bowl with water, and washed himself meticulously. Then he disappeared for the whole day, making a brief appearance only at noon to collect his soup in the same bowl. In the evening he came back for dinner, ate, went out again, re-entered soon afterwards with a chamber pot, placed it in the corner behind the stove, sat there for a few moments, left again with the pot, came back without it, climbed up quietly to his own place, punctiliously adjusted the blankets and pillow, and slept until the morning without changing position.

A few days after my arrival, I saw with discomfort a well-known face appear: the pathetic and disagreeable shape of Kleine Kiepura, the mascot of Buna-Monowitz. They all knew him at Buna; he was the youngest of the prisoners, no more than twelve years old. Everything was irregular about him, beginning with his presence in Lager, which normally children did not enter alive. No-one knew how or why he had been admitted, yet at the same time everybody knew only too well. His position there was irregular, because he did not march to work, but lived in semi-isolation in the officials' Block; moreover, his whole appearance was strikingly irregular. He had grown too much and badly; enormously long arms and legs stuck out from his squat, short body, like those of a spider; below his pale face, whose features were not lacking in infantile grace, a huge jaw jutted out, more prominent than his nose. Kleine Kiepura was the attendant and protégé of the Lager-Kapo, the Kapo of all the Kapos.

Nobody loved him, except his protector. In the shadow of authority, well fed and dressed, exempt from work, he had led until the very end the ambiguous and frivolous existence of a favourite, amid a web of denunciations and twisted affections; his name, wrongly I hope, was always whispered in the most notorious anonymous denunciations to the Political Bureau and to the S.S. Hence all feared him and shrank from him.

But now the Lager-Kapo, deprived of all power, was marching towards the West, and Kleine Kiepura, recovering from a slight illness, shared our lot. He was given a bunk and a bowl, and he inserted himself into our limbo. Henek and I addressed only a few cautious words to him, hindered as we were by diffidence and hostile compassion; but he barely replied. He stayed silent for two days; he sat huddled in his bunk, staring into space with his fists tight against his chest. Then all of a sudden he began to speak – and we longed for his silence. Kleine Kiepura spoke as if in a dream: and his dream was of a success story, of becoming a Kapo. It was difficult to tell if it was madness or a puerile sinister game; endlessly, from the height of his bunk immediately below the ceiling, the boy sang and whistled the marches of Buna, the brutal rhythms that ruled our tired steps every morning and evening; he shouted imperious commands in German at a troop of non-existent slaves.

'Get up, swine, understand? Make your beds, quickly;

26

clean your shoes. All in line, lice inspection, feet inspection! Show your feet, scum! Dirty again, you shit-heap! Watch out, I'm not joking. If I catch you once more, it's the crematorium for you!' Then, yelling in the manner of German soldiers: 'Fall in! Dressed! Covered! Collar down; in step, keep time! Hands in line with the seams of your trousers!' And then again, after a pause, in an arrogant and stridulous voice: 'This isn't a sanatorium! This is a German Lager, its name is Auschwitz, and no one leaves except through the Chimney. If you like it, all right; if you don't, all you have to do is touch the electric wire!'

Kleine Kiepura disappeared after a few days, to everybody's relief. His presence among us, weak and ill, but full of the timid and flickering joy of our new-found liberty, offended like that of a corpse, and the compassion he aroused in us was mixed with horror. We tried in vain to tear him from his delirium: the infection of the Lager had gained too much ground.

The two Polish girls, who carried out the duties of nurse (pretty badly), were named Hanka and Jadzia. Hanka was an ex-Kapo, as one could tell from her unshaven hair, and even more surely from her insolent manner. She could hardly have been more than twenty-four; she was of average height, with a dark complexion and hard vulgar features. In that purgatory, full of past and present sufferings, of hopes and pity, she spent her days in front of the mirror, filing her nails, or strutting in front of the indifferent and ironical Henek.

She was, or considered herself, of a higher social standing than Jadzia: but it needed very little indeed to surpass in authority so humble a creature. Jadzia was a small and timid girl, of a sickly-rosy colour; but her sheath of anaemic flesh was tormented, torn apart from inside, convulsed by a continual secret tempest. She had a desire, an urge, an impelling need of a man, of any man, at once, of all men. Every male

27

who crossed her path attracted her; attracted her materially, heavily, as a magnet attracts iron. Jadzia stared at him with bewitched and stupefied eyes, she rose from her corner, advanced towards him with the uncertain step of a somnambulist, sought contact with him; if the man then drew away, she followed him at a distance, in silence, for a few yards, then, with her eyes lowered, returned to her inertia; if the man waited for her, Jadzia wrapped herself around him, incorporated him, took possession of him, with the blind, mute, tremulous, slow, but sure movements which amoebae show under the microscope.

Her first and principal objective was naturally Henek; but Henek did not want her, he derided and insulted her. But, being the practical boy he was, he had not lost interest in the case, and had mentioned it to Noah, his great friend.

Noah did not live in our dormitory; in fact he lived nowhere and everywhere. He was a nomad, a free man, rejoicing in the air he breathed and the ground he trod upon. He was Scheissminister of free Auschwitz, Minister of latrines and cesspits; but notwithstanding this monatto-like post of his (which in any case he had assumed voluntarily) there was nothing sordid about him, or if there were anything, it was cancelled out by the impetus of his vital energy. Noah was a young Pantagruel, as strong as a horse, voracious and lecherous. As Jadzia wanted all men, so Noah wanted all women; but while the feeble Jadzia limited herself to throwing out her tenuous threads, like a rock-mollusc, Noah, a high-flying bird, cruised along all the roads of the camp from dawn to dusk, on the seat of his repugnant cart, cracking his whip and singing at the top of his voice; the cart stopped before the entrance of each Block, and while his troop, filthy and stinking, hurried, cursing, through their repulsive task, Noah wandered around the feminine dormitories like an oriental prince, dressed in an arabesque many-coloured coat, full of patches and braid. His encounters were like so many hurricanes. He was the friend of all men and the lover of all women. The deluge was over; in the black sky of Auschwitz, Noah saw the rainbow shine out, and the world was his, to repopulate.

Frau Vitta (or rather Frau Vita, as every Italian called her*), on the other hand, loved all human beings with a love both simple and fraternal. Frau Vita, with her ruined figure and clear gentle face, was a young widow from Trieste, half Jewish, a survivor of Birkenau. She spent many hours beside my bed, speaking to me of a thousand things at the same time with Triestine volubility, laughing and crying. She was in good health, but deeply wounded, ulcerated, by what she had undergone and seen in a year of Lager, and during those last gruesome days. In fact, she had been 'commandeered' for the transport of corpses, of lumps of corpses, of wretched anonymous remains, and these final images weighed upon her like a mountain; she sought to exorcise them, to wash herself clean of them, throwing herself headlong into a tumultuous activity. She was the only person to bother about the invalids and the children; she did it with frantic compassion, and when she still had free time she washed the floors and windows with wild fury, rinsed the bowls and glasses noisily, ran around the dormitories to carry real or fictitious messages; then she came back exhausted, and sat panting on my bunk, with tearful eyes, starved of words, of intimacy, of human warmth. In the evening, when all the jobs of the day were over, incapable of enduring solitude, she suddenly jumped up from her bunk, and danced by herself between the bunks, to the sound of her own songs, affectionately clasping an imaginary man to her breast.

It was Frau Vita who closed André's and Antoine's eyes. They were two young peasants from the Vosges, both my companions for the ten days of the interregnum, both ill with diphtheria. I seemed to have known them for centuries. With

* 'Vita' in Italian means 'life'.

strange parallelism, they were simultaneously struck by a form of dysentery, which soon showed itself to be extremely serious, of tubercular origin; in a few days the scales of their fate tipped down. They were in two neighbouring bunks, they did not complain, they endured the atrocious colic with clenched teeth, without understanding its mortal nature; they spoke only to each other, timidly, and they never asked anyone for help. André was the first to go, while he was speaking, in mid-sentence, as a candle goes out. For two days no-one arrived to take him away; the children came to look at him with bewildered curiosity, then continued to play in their corner.

Antoine remained silent and alone, wholly shut in a suspense that transformed him. His state of nutrition was reasonable, but in two days he underwent a metamorphosis of dissolution, as if sucked up by his companion. Together with Frau Vita we managed to get a doctor, after many vain attempts; I asked him, in German, if there was anything to be done, if there was any hope, and I counselled him not to speak in French. He replied in Yiddish, with a brief phrase I did not understand; then he translated into German: '*Sein Kamerad ruft ihn*', 'His companion is calling him'. Antoine obeyed the call that same evening. They were not yet twenty, and they had been in the Lager only one month.

Finally Olga came, in a night full of silence, to bring me the dismal news of the Birkenau camp, and of the fate of the women deported with me. I had been waiting for her for many days; I did not know her personally, but Frau Vita, who, despite sanitary injunctions, also frequented patients in other wards in search of troubles to alleviate and of impassioned conversations, had informed us of our respective presences, and had organized the illegal meeting in the depth of the night while everyone was sleeping.

Olga was a Jewish Croat partisan, who in 1942 had fled to Piedmont with her family and had been interned there; she belonged to that flood of thousands of foreign Jews who had found hospitality, and a brief peace, in the paradoxical Italy of those years, officially anti-Semitic. She was a woman of great intelligence and culture, strong, beautiful and with insight: deported to Birkenau, she had survived there, alone of her family.

She spoke Italian perfectly; from reasons of gratitude and temperament, she had soon become a friend of the Italian women in the camp, and in particular of those who had been deported in the same train as I. She told me their story by candlelight, with her eyes fixed on the ground. The furtive light illumined only her face in the darkness, accentuating its precocious lines, and transforming it into a tragic mask. A handkerchief covered her head; she untied it at one point and the mask became as macabre as a skull. Olga's cranium was bare, covered only with a short grey down.

They had all died. All the children and all the old people had died immediately. Of the 550 people of whom I had lost trace when I entered the Lager, only twenty-nine women had been admitted to the Birkenau camp: of these, five alone had survived. Vanda had died by gas, fully conscious, in the month of October; Olga herself had procured two sleeping tablets for her, but they had not proved sufficient.

3. The Greek

TOWARDS THE END of February, after a month in bed, I was not yet cured, and indeed began to feel but little improvement. I had a clear impression that I would not regain my health and my strength until I stood upright again (albeit with difficulty), and put shoes on my feet. So, on one of the rare days when the doctor called, I asked him to let me out. The doctor examined me, or pretended to do so; he noted that the desquamation of the scarlet fever had finished; he told me that as far as he was concerned I could go; he warned me, absurdly, not to expose myself to fatigue or cold, and he wished me good luck.

I cut myself a pair of socks from a blanket, grabbed as many jackets and pairs of trousers as I could find (for no other clothing was to hand), said good-bye to Frau Vita and Henek, and went out.

I stood on my feet somewhat shakily. Immediately outside the door, there was a Soviet officer; he photographed me and gave me five cigarettes. A little farther on, I was unable to avoid a fellow in civilian dress, who was hunting for men to clear away the snow; he captured me, deaf to my protests, gave me a spade, and attached me to a squad of shovellers.

I offered him the five cigarettes but he refused them with contempt. He was an ex-Kapo, and had naturally remained in office; who else in fact could have managed to make people like us clear the snow? I tried to shovel, but it was physically impossible. If I could get round the corner, no-one would see me any more, but first I had to free myself of the spade; it would have been interesting to sell it, but I did not know to whom; and to carry it with me even for a few steps was dangerous. There was not enough snow to bury it. In the end I dropped it through a cellar window, and I found myself free again.

I walked into a Block; there was a guardian, an old Hungarian, who did not want to let me enter, but the cigarettes convinced him. Inside it was warm, full of smoke and noise and unknown faces; but in the evening they gave soup to me as well. I was hoping for a few days of rest and of gradual training for an active life, but I did not know that I had tripped up badly. No later than the following morning, I got caught up in a Russian transport convoy towards a mysterious transit camp.

I cannot say that I remember exactly how and when my Greek sprang up from nowhere. In those days and in those parts, soon after the front had passed by, a high wind was blowing over the face of the earth; the world around us seemed to have returned to primeval Chaos, and was swarming with scalene, defective, abnormal human specimens; each of them bestirred himself, with blind or deliberate movements, in anxious search of his own place, of his own sphere, as the particles of the four elements are described as doing in the verse-cosmogonies of the Ancients.

I too, swept up by the whirlwind, found myself, one bitter night, after a heavy snowfall, loaded on to a horse-drawn military cart many hours before dawn, together with a dozen unknown companions. The cold was intense; the sky, thick with stars, slowly lightened in the east, promising one of those marvellous daybreaks of the plain, which, at the time of our slavery, we had watched interminably in the Roll-call square of the Lager.

Our guide and escort was a Russian soldier. He sat in front singing full-throatedly to the stars, and every now and again spoke to the horses in that strangely affectionate way that Russians have, with gentle inflections and long modulated phrases. Naturally, we had asked him about our destination, but we got nothing comprehensible from him, except – as far as we could gather from certain rhythmic puffings of his and from the movement of his elbows bent like piston-rods – that his task was limited to taking us as far as a railway.

This was in fact what happened. As the sun rose, the cart stopped at the foot of an embankment which carried the railway lines, interrupted and destroyed for about fifty yards by a recent bombardment. The soldier pointed to one of the two sections, helped us climb down from the cart (it was necessary: the journey had lasted nearly two hours, the cart was small, and many of us, because of the uncomfortable position and the penetrating cold, were so numb as to be unable to move), took leave of us with jovial incomprehensible words, turned the horses round, and departed, singing sweetly.

The sun, which had barely risen, had disappeared behind a veil of mist; from the top of the railway embankment we could only see an interminable flat, deserted countryside, buried under the snow, without a roof, without a tree. More hours passed; not one of us had a watch.

As I have already said, we were about a dozen. There was a *Reichsdeutscher* who, like many other 'Aryan' Germans, had assumed relatively courteous and frankly ambiguous attitudes after the liberation (this was an amusing metamorphosis, which I had already seen happen in others, sometimes gradually, sometimes in a few minutes at the first appearance of the new lords of the Red Star, on whose large faces it was easy to read the tendency not to split hairs). There were two tall, thin brothers, Viennese Jews about fifty years old, silent and cautious like all the old Häftlinge; an officer of the regular Yugoslav Army, who seemed as if he had not yet succeeded in throwing off the compliance and inertia of the Lager, and who looked at us with empty eyes. There was a sort of human wreck, of indefinable age, who spoke ceaselessly to himself in Yiddish; one of the many whom the ferocious life of the camp

34

had half destroyed, and then left to their fate, sealed up (and perhaps protected) by a thick armour of insensitivity or open madness. And finally there was the Greek, with whom destiny was to unite me for an unforgettable week of vagabondage.

His name was Mordo Nahum, and at first sight he seemed nothing exceptional, except for his shoes (of leather, almost new, of elegant design: a real portent, given the time and the place), and the sack that he carried on his back, which was of conspicuous size and corresponding weight, as I myself was to ascertain in the following days. Besides his own language, he spoke Spanish (like all Jews from Salonica), French, a halting Italian but with a good accent, and, as I found out later, Turkish, Bulgarian and a little Albanian. He was about forty; of fairly tall stature, he walked with curved shoulders, his head pushed forward like a myope. Red of hair and skin, he had large pale watery eyes and a great curved nose, which gave his whole body a rapacious yet halting appearance, like a nightbird surprised by light, or a shark outside its natural environment.

He was recovering from some indeterminate illness, which caused attacks of extremely high, enervating fever; in the first nights of the journey he still sometimes fell into a state of prostration, with attacks of shivering and delirium. Although we did not feel particularly attracted to each other, we were drawn together by having two languages in common, and by the fact, quite noticeable in the circumstances, that we were the only two Mediterraneans in the small group.

The waiting was interminable; we were hungry and cold, and we were forced to stand or lie down in the snow, because there was no roof or shelter as far as the eye could see. It must have been nearly midday when, heralded from afar by the puffing and smoke, the hand of civilization was stretched out to us charitably in the form of an emaciated string of three or four goods trucks dragged by a small locomotive, such as is used in normal times for shunting wagons.

The train stopped in front of us, at the end of the interrupted line. We were unable to gain any sensible information from the few Polish peasants who got out; they looked at us with closed faces, and avoided us as if we were pestiferous. In fact, we were, probably in the strict sense of the word, and in any case our aspect could hardly have been pleasing: but we had misguidedly hoped for a more cordial welcome from the first 'civilians' we met after our liberation. We all climbed into one of the trucks, and the small train left almost at once in the opposite direction, pushed and no longer pulled by the toy locomotive. At the next stopping place two peasant women climbed on; once the first diffidence and linguistic obstacles had been overcome, we learnt from them some important geographical facts, and some news which, if true, sounded little less than disastrous to our ears.

The break in the railway line was a little way from a locality named Neu Berun, which had formerly been the junction for a branch line, later destroyed, to Auschwitz. The two sections which started from the interruption led to Katowice (to the west), and to Cracow (to the east). Both of these localities lay about forty miles from Neu Berun, which, in the frightful conditions in which the war had left the line, meant at least two days' journey, with an unspecified number of stops and changes. The train on which we found ourselves was travelling towards Cracow; until a few days before, the Russians had gathered an enormous number of ex-prisoners at Cracow, and now all the barracks, schools, hospitals and convents were overflowing with people in a condition of desperate need. The very streets of Cracow, according to our informers, were swarming with men and women of all races. who in a moment had transformed themselves into smugglers, clandestine merchants, even into thieves and bandits.

For several days now, the ex-prisoners had been concentrated into other camps, around Katowice. The two women were amazed to find us travelling towards Cracow, where, they said, the Russian garrison itself was suffering from hunger. After they had heard our story they consulted briefly, then they declared themselves convinced that it must simply have been a mistake on the part of our escort, the Russian cart-driver, who, with little knowledge of the country, had directed us towards the eastern section instead of towards the western.

The news plunged us into a riddle of doubts and anxiety. We had hoped for a short and safe journey, towards a camp equipped to receive us, towards an acceptable substitute for our homes; and this hope formed part of a far greater hope, that of an upright and just world, miraculously re-established on its natural foundations after an eternity of upheavals, of errors and massacres, after our long patient wait. It was a naïve hope, like all those that rest on too sharp a division between good and evil, between past and future, but it was on this that we were living. That first crack, and the other inevitable ones, small and large, that followed it, were for us a cause of grief, the more hardly felt because they were unforeseen; for one does not dream for years, for decades, of a better world, without representing it as perfect.

It was not so; something had happened that only the few wise ones among us had foreseen. Liberty, the improbable, the impossible liberty, so far removed from Auschwitz that we had only dared to hope for it in our dreams, had come, but it had not taken us to the Promised Land. It was around us, but in the form of a pitiless deserted plain. More trials, more toil, more hunger, more cold, more fears awaited us.

I had been fasting now for twenty-four hours. We were sitting on the wooden floor of the truck, huddled together to protect ourselves from the cold; the railway lines were loose, and at every bump our heads, unsteady on our necks, knocked against the wooden planks of the walls. I felt exhausted, not only physically; like an athlete who has run for hours, using up all his own resources, those of nature

37

first, and then those that he squeezes out, that he creates from nothing in moments of extreme need; like an athlete who arrives at his goal, and who, in the act of falling spent to the ground, is brutally hauled to his feet, and forced to start running again, in the dark, towards another goal of unknown distance.

The train travelled slowly. In the evening dark, apparently deserted villages emerged; then total night came down, atrociously cold, without light in heaven or on earth. Only the bumping of the truck prevented us from drifting into a sleep which the cold would have rendered mortal. After interminable hours of travel, perhaps about three o'clock at night, we finally stopped at a wrecked, dark, little station. The Greek was delirious; of the others, none wanted to get down from the truck, some from fear, some from sheer inertia, some in the hope that the train would leave soon. I got down, and wandered into the dark with my ridiculous baggage until I saw a small lighted window. It was the telegraph hut, packed with people: there was a lighted stove. I entered cautiously, like a stray dog, ready to disappear at the first sign of a threat, but nobody bothered about me. I threw myself on the floor and fell asleep at once, as one learns to do in the Lager.

I woke up some hours later at dawn. The hut was empty. The telegraphist saw me raise my head, and placed an enormous slice of bread and cheese beside me on the ground. I was startled (apart from being half paralysed by the cold and sleep) and I fear I did not thank him. I pushed the food into my stomach and went outside; the train had not moved. In the truck, my companions were lying besotted; when they saw me they shook themselves, all except the Yugoslav, who strove to move in vain. The cold and immobility had paralysed his legs; when we touched him he shouted and groaned. We had to massage him for a long time, and then to move his limbs cautiously, as one inches a rusty mechanism.

It had been a terrible night for everyone, perhaps the worst of our whole exile. I spoke to the Greek about it; we agreed to join forces so as to avoid at all costs another freezing night, which we felt we should not survive.

I think that the Greek, thanks to my nocturnal outing, had somehow overestimated my qualities of *'débrouillard et démerdard'*, as they were elegantly described at the time. As for myself, I confess that I was impressed mainly by his big sack and his quality of a Salonikite, which, as everyone in Auschwitz knew, was equivalent to a guarantee of highly skilled mercantile ability, and of knowing how to get oneself out of any situation. Sympathy, bilateral, and esteem, unilateral, came later.

The train left again, and by a tortuous and vague route led us to a place called Szczakowa. Here the Polish Red Cross had established a marvellous field-kitchen; a quite substantial hot soup was distributed at all hours of the day and night, and to anyone, without distinction, who presented himself. A miracle that none of us would have dared to dream of in our most audacious dreams: in a certain sense, the Lager upside down. I do not remember the behaviour of my companions; as for myself, I was so voracious that the Polish sisters, used as they were to the famished clientele of the place, crossed themselves.

We left again in the afternoon. The sun was out. Our poor train stopped at dusk, in trouble; far away the spires of Cracow glowed red. The Greek and I got down from the truck and went to interrogate the engine-driver, who stood in the middle of the snow, busy and dirty, fighting long jets of steam that shot out from some burst pipe. *'Masheena kaputt,'* he replied to us epigraphically. We were no longer slaves, we were no longer protected, we had left our tutelage. For us the hour of trial was sounding.

The Greek, revived by the hot soup of Szczakowa, felt quite strong. *'On y va?'* – *'On y va.'* So we left the train and our perplexed companions, whom we were never to see again, and we started out on foot in the problematical search for human kind.

At his peremptory request I shouldered the famous bundle. In vain I had tried to protest. 'But it's your stuff!' 'Exactly, because it is mine. I organized it and you carry it. That's the division of work. Later you too will profit from it.' So we started off, he first and I second, on the hard snow of a minor road; the sun had gone down.

I have spoken already of the Greek's shoes; as for myself, I was wearing a pair of curious foot-coverings which in Italy I had only seen worn by priests: of extremely delicate leather, reaching higher than the ankle, without laces, but with two large clasps, and two lateral patches of elastic fabric which should have ensured that they remained tight-fitting. I was also wearing four pairs of Häftling-style cloth trousers on top of each other, a cotton shirt, a jacket, also striped – and that was all. My baggage consisted of a blanket and a cardboard box in which I had formerly kept a few pieces of bread, but which was now empty. The Greek eyed the whole lot with unconcealed contempt and annoyance.

We had deceived ourselves grossly about the distance from Cracow: we should have to walk at least four miles. After about twenty minutes, my shoes were finished; the sole of one of them had come off, and the other began to unstitch itself. Until then the Greek had maintained a pregnant silence; when he saw me put down the sack and sit by the side of the road to contemplate the disaster, he asked me:

'How old are you?'

'Twenty-five,' I replied.

'What do you do?'

'I'm a chemist.'

'Then you're a fool,' he said calmly. 'A man who has no shoes is a fool.'

He was a great Greek. Few times in my life, before or after, have I felt such concrete wisdom weigh upon me. There was little to say in reply. The validity of the argument was manifest, plain: the two shapeless pieces of trash on my feet, and the two shining marvels on his. There was no justification. I was no longer a slave; but after my first steps on the path of liberty, here was I seated by the road, with my feet in my hands clumsy and useless like the broken-down locomotive we had just left. Was I really entitled to my liberty? The Greek seemed to doubt it.

'... But I had scarlet fever, a high temperature, I was in the sick bay; the shoe store was a long way off, it was forbidden to go near it, and anyway they said that it had been sacked by the Poles. And didn't I have the right to believe that the Russians would have provided?'

'Words,' said the Greek. 'Anyone can talk. I had a temperature of 104, and I didn't know if it was day or night; but one thing I did know, that I needed shoes and other things; so I got up, and I went as far as the store to study the situation. There was a Russian with a sten-gun in front of the door, but I wanted the shoes, and so I walked to the back, I broke open a small window and I entered. So I got my shoes, and also the sack, and everything that is inside the sack, which will prove useful later on. That is foresight; yours is stupidity. It's a failure to understand the reality of things.'

'Now it's you who are just talking,' said I. 'I may have made a mistake, but now the problem is how to reach Cracow before nightfall, with or without shoes'; and so saying I fumbled around with numbed fingers, and with bits of wire I found on the road, trying to tie the soles to the uppers, at least provisionally.

'Hold it; that'll be no use at all.' He gave me two pieces of robust cloth that he had dragged out of his bundle, and showed me how to pack together shoes and feet, firmly enough at least to hobble along. Then we proceeded in silence.

The suburbs of Cracow were anonymous and squalid. The roads were wholly deserted: the shops were empty, all the doors and windows were barred or smashed. We reached the terminus of a tram line; I hesitated, because we had no money to pay the fare, but the Greek said: 'Climb on, then we'll see.' The tram was empty; after a quarter of an hour the driver arrived, but not the conductor (from which we see that once more the Greek was right; as we shall see, he was to prove right in all the succeeding situations, except one); we left, and during the journey discovered with joy that one of the passengers who had climbed on in the meantime was a Frenchman. He explained to us that he was staying in an old convent, which our tram would soon pass; at the following stop, we should find a barracks requisitioned by the Russians and full of Italian soldiers. My heart rejoiced; I had found a home.

In reality, things did not all go so smoothly. At first, the Polish guard on duty at the barracks told us abruptly to go away. 'Where?' 'What do I care? Away from here, anywhere.' After much insistence and begging, he was finally induced to go and call an Italian sergeant, on whom the decision to admit other guests clearly depended. It was not easy, he explained to us; the barracks were already bursting, rations were limited; he conceded that I was an Italian, but I was not a soldier; as for my companion, he was Greek, and it was impossible to put him in with veterans of the Greek and Albanian campaigns; disorders and fights would inevitably result. I countered with my best eloquence, and with genuine tears in my eyes; I guaranteed that we would only stay one night (and I thought to myself: once inside . . .) and that the Greek spoke Italian well and in any case would open his mouth as little as possible. My arguments were weak, and I was aware of it, but the Greek knew how to work all the skives in the world, and while I was speaking he was routing about in the sack hanging on my back. At a certain point he pushed me aside, and in silence placed under the nose of the Cerberus a dazzling tin of pork, embellished with a many-coloured label, and with futile instructions in six languages on the correct way to handle the contents. So we won a roof and a bed at Cracow.

It was already night. Contrary to what the sergeant had led us to believe, the most sumptuous abundance reigned inside the barracks; there were lighted stoves, candles and acetylene lamps, food and drink, and straw to sleep on. The Italians were distributed ten or twelve to a dormitory, but we at Monowitz had been two per cubic yard. They were wearing good military clothing, thick jackets, many of them had wrist watches, all of them had hair shining with brilliantine; they were noisy, cheerful and obliging and overwhelmed us with kindness. As for the Greek, they virtually carried him in triumph. A Greek! A Greek has come! The news rang from dormitory to dormitory, and in a short time a festive crowd gathered around my surly partner. They spoke Greek, some of them with ease, these veterans of the most compassionate military occupation that history records: they talked of places and events with colourful sympathy, in a chivalrous tacit recognition of the desperate valour of the invaded country. But there was something more, which opened the way for them; mine was no ordinary Greek, he was visibly a master, an authority, a super-Greek. In a few moments of conversation, he had accomplished a miracle, he had created an atmosphere.

He possessed the right equipment; he could speak Italian, and (what matters more, and what is missing in many Italians themselves) he knew of what to speak in Italian. He amazed me; he showed himself an expert about girls and spaghetti, Juventus* and lyrical music, the war and blennorrhoea, wine and the black market, motor-bikes and spivs.

* A leading Italian football club.

43

Mordo Nahum, so laconic with me, in a brief time became the pivot of the evening. I realized that his eloquence, his successful attempt at *captatio benevolentiae*, did not derive solely from opportunist considerations. He too had fought in the Greek campaign, with the rank of sergeant; on the other side of the front, naturally, but this detail at the moment seemed trifling to everybody. He had been at Tepeleni, many Italians had also been there; like them he had suffered cold, hunger, mud and bombardments, and in the end, like them, he had been captured by the Germans. He was a colleague, a fellow-soldier.

He told curious stories of the war; of how, after the Germans had broken through the front, he had found himself with six of his soldiers ransacking the first floor of a bombed and abandoned villa, searching for provisions; he had heard suspicious noises on the floor below, had cautiously climbed down the stairs with his sten-gun at the ready, and had met an Italian sergeant, who with six soldiers was doing exactly the same thing on the ground floor. The Italian in turn had levelled his gun, but the Greek had pointed out that in those conditions a gun fight would have been particularly stupid, that they all found themselves, Greeks and Italians, in the same boat, and that he did not see why they should not make a small separate local peace and continue their researches in their respective occupied territories – to which proposal the Italian had rapidly agreed.

For me too he was a revelation. I knew that he was nothing but a rogue, a merchant, expert in deceit and lacking in scruples, selfish and cold; yet I felt blossom out in him, encouraged by the sympathy of the audience, a warmth, an unsuspected humanity, singular but genuine, rich with promise.

Late at night, heaven knows how, a flask of wine suddenly appeared. It was the *coup de grâce*: for me everything sank celestially into a warm purple fog, and I barely managed to drag myself on all fours to the straw bed that the Italians,

44

with maternal care, had prepared in a corner for the Greek and myself.

Dawn had barely risen when the Greek woke me. Alas! Where had last night's jovial guest disappeared to? The Greek who stood in front of me was hard, secretive, taciturn. 'Get up,' he said in a tone of voice that admitted no reply, 'put your shoes on, get the sack and let's go.'

'Go where?'

'To work, to the market. Do you think it's a nice thing to be supported?'

I felt wholly opposed to this argument. It seemed to me, besides being convenient, extremely natural and also pleasant that someone should keep me; I had found the explosion of national solidarity, or rather of spontaneous humanity, the evening before both enjoyable and exhilarating. Even more, full as I was of self-pity, it seemed to me just, good, that the world should at last pity me. Moreover, I had no shoes, I was ill, I was cold, I was tired; and finally, in the name of all the gods, what the hell could I do at the market?

I disclosed all these considerations, obvious to me. But, *'c'est pas des raisons d'homme,'* he replied sharply; I was forced to realize that I had infringed an important moral principle of his, that he was seriously scandalized, that on this point he was not prepared for compromise or discussion. Moral codes, all of them, are rigid by definition; they do not admit blurrings, compromises, or reciprocal contaminations. They are to be accepted or rejected *en bloc*. This is one of the principal reasons why man is gregarious and searches more or less consciously for the company not of his generic neighbour, but only of someone who shares his profound beliefs (or lack of them). I was obliged to recognize, with disappointment and amazement, that Mordo Nahum was such a man, a man of deep-rooted beliefs, and, what is more, beliefs far removed from mine. Now everyone knows how awkward it is to do business, in fact to live together, with an ideological opponent.

The basis of his ethic was work, which to him was a sacred duty, but which he understood in a very wide sense. To him, work included everything, but with the condition that it should bring profit without limiting liberty. The concept of work thus included, as well as certain permissible activities, smuggling, theft and fraud (not robbery; he was not a violent man). On the other hand he considered reprehensible, because humiliating, all activities which did not involve initiative or risk, or which presupposed a discipline and a hierarchy; any relationship of employment, any services, even if they were well paid, he lumped together as 'servile work'. But it was not servile work to plough your own field, or to sell false antiques to tourists at a port.

As for the more elevated activities of the spirit, as for creative work, I soon understood that the Greek was divided. These were delicate judgements, to be made on the merits of each case; it was permissible for example to pursue success for its own sake, even by selling false paintings or literary trash, or, more generally, by harming one's neighbour; it was reprehensible obstinately to pursue an unprofitable ideal; it was sinful to withdraw from the world in contemplation; the path of the man who dedicated himself to meditation and the acquisition of wisdom, on the other hand, was permissible, in fact commendable – so long as he did not believe that he had the right to receive his bread free from mankind, for wisdom was also merchandise, which could and should be exchanged.

Since Mordo Nahum was no fool, he clearly realized that these principles might not be shared by individuals of a different origin and formation, and in particular by me; he was however firmly persuaded of them, and it was his ambition to put them into practice, to demonstrate their general validity.

In conclusion, my proposal to wait quietly for food from the Russians could only appear detestable to him; because it was 'unearned bread'; because it implied a relationship of

46

subjection; and because every form of order, of structure, was suspect to him, whether it brought a loaf of bread a day, or a monthly pay-packet.

So I followed the Greek to the market, not really because I was convinced by his arguments, but mainly through inertia and curiosity. The evening before, when I was already navigating in a sea of vinous vapours, he had diligently inquired about the location, customs, tariffs, supply and demand of the free market of Cracow, and his duty now called him.

We left, he with the sack (which I carried), I in my disintegrating shoes, which turned each step into a problem. The market of Cracow had blossomed out spontaneously, as soon as the front had passed by, and in a few days it had invaded an entire suburb. Everything was bought and sold there, and the whole city centred on it; townsfolk were selling furniture, books, paintings, clothes and silver; peasant women, padded out like mattresses, offered meat, poultry, eggs, cheese; boys and girls, with noses and cheeks reddened by the icy wind, searched for tobacco-addicts to buy their ration, which the Soviet military administration distributed with extravagant munificence (ten ounces a month to everybody, including babies).

With joy I met a group of compatriots: quick-witted folk, three soldiers and a girl, jovial and spendthrift, who carried on an excellent business in those days of cold and hunger with a sort of hot fritter, cooked with unusual ingredients in a doorway nearby.

After a preliminary survey, the Greek decided on shirts. Were we partners? Well then, he would contribute the capital and business experience; I, my (feeble) knowledge of German and the physical work. 'Off you go,' he told me, 'wander around all the stalls where they are selling shirts, ask how much they cost, reply that it's too much, then report back to me. Don't let yourself be noticed too much.' Reluctantly I

47

prepared to carry out this market research; I still harboured a fossil hunger, cold and inertia, and at the same time curiosity, lightheartedness and a new and sapid willingness to converse, to open up human contacts, to parade and squander my immeasurable liberty. But the Greek, behind the back of my would-be vendors, followed me with severe eye; hurry up, damn you, time is money, and business is business.

I came back from my investigation with some comparative prices, which the Greek noted mentally; and with a fair number of disordered philological oddments: that one says something like *koshoola* for a shirt; that Polish numbers resemble Greek ones; that for 'how much' and 'what time is it' one says something like *eela kostooya* and *ktoora gojeena*; a termination of the genitive in *-ago* that clarified the sense of some Polish oaths I had often heard in the Lager; and other scraps of information which filled me with a foolish and puerile joy.

The Greek was calculating to himself. A shirt could be sold for fifty to one hundred zloty; an egg cost five or six zloty; for ten zloty, according to the Italian fritter-mongers, one could eat soup and another course at the soup-kitchen behind the cathedral. The Greek decided to sell only one of the three shirts he owned, and to eat at the soup-kitchen; the surplus would be invested in eggs. Then we would see what to do.

So he gave me the shirt, and ordered me to hold it up and shout: 'a shirt, gentlemen, a shirt.' For 'shirt', I was already documented; as for 'gentlemen', I believed that the correct form was *Panovye*, which I had heard used a few minutes before by my rivals and which I interpreted as a plural vocative of *Pan*, gentleman. As for this last term, I had no doubts: it is to be found in an important dialogue in *The Brothers Karamazov*. It really must have been the correct word, as various clients addressed me in Polish, asking me incomprehensible questions about the shirt. I was in difficulties; the

Greek intervened authoritatively, pushed me aside and personally conducted the negotiations, which were long and laborious, but which ended happily. At the purchaser's request, the consignment of the article took place, not in the public square, but in a doorway.

Seventy zloty, equivalent to seven meals or a dozen eggs. I don't know about the Greek; as for myself, I had not possessed so large a sum of foodstuffs all at one time for fourteen months. But did I really possess them? It seemed highly doubtful; the Greek had pocketed the sum silently, and his whole attitude led one to understand that he intended to keep the administration of the profits to himself.

We wandered round the egg-stalls, where we learnt that hard-boiled and raw eggs sold at the same price. We bought six for dinner: the Greek proceeded to their purchase with extreme care, choosing the largest after detailed comparisons and much perplexity and changes of mind, wholly insensitive to the disapproving looks of the seller.

The soup-kitchen was behind the cathedral; it remained only to determine which, of the many and beautiful churches of Cracow, was the cathedral. Whom could one ask, and how? A priest walked by; I would ask the priest. Now the priest, young and of benign appearance, understood neither French nor German; as a result, for the first and only time in my post-scholastic career, I reaped the fruits of years of classical studies, carrying on the most extravagant and chaotic of conversations in Latin. After the initial request for information (*Pater optime, ubi est mensa pauperorum?*), we began to speak confusedly of everything, of my being a Jew, of the Lager (*castra?* Better: Lager, only too likely to be understood by everybody), of Italy, of the danger of speaking German in public (which I was to understand soon after, by direct experience), and of innumerable other things, to which the unusual dress of the language gave a curious air of the remotest past.

I had completely forgotten the hunger and the cold, so true is it that the need for human contact is to be numbered among the primordial needs. I had also forgotten the Greek; but he had not forgotten me, and he emerged brutally after a few minutes, interrupting the conversation pitilessly. It was not that he was incapable of human contact, or that he did not understand its value (I had seen that the evening before in the barracks); but it was something for outside office hours, for holidays, something supplementary, not to be mixed up with the serious and strenuous business that was daily work. To my feeble protests, he replied only with a morose look. We walked on; the Greek was silent for a long time, then, as a conclusive judgement on my collaboration, he said to me in a thoughtful tone: '*Je n'ai pas encore compris si tu es idiot ou fainéant.*'

By following the priest's valuable directions, we reached the soup-kitchen. It was a somewhat depressing place, but warm and full of voluptuous smells. The Greek ordered two soups and only one ration of beans with lard; this was the punishment for my indecorous and fatuous behaviour in the morning. He was angry; but after he had gulped down his soup he softened perceptibly, so much so as to leave me a good quarter of his beans. Outside it had begun to snow, and a vicious wind was blowing. Whether from pity at the sight of my striped clothes, or from indifference to the regulations, the kitchen staff left us in peace for a good part of the afternoon to meditate and make plans for the future. The Greek's mood seemed to have changed; perhaps his fever had returned, or perhaps, after the bargains of the morning, he felt that he was on holiday. In fact he was in a benevolently pedagogic mood; as the hours slowly passed, the tone of his discourse grew gradually warmer, and on a parallel plane the tie that united us changed: from owner-slave at midday, to employer-employee at one o'clock, from master-disciple at two o'clock, to elder brother-younger brother at three o'clock.

The discourse came back to my shoes, which neither of us, for different reasons, could forget. He explained to me that to be without shoes is a very serious fault. When war is waging, one has to think of two things before all others: in the first place of one's shoes, in the second place of food to eat; and not vice versa, as the common herd believes, because he who has shoes can search for food, but the inverse is not true. 'But the war is over,' I objected: and I thought it was over, as did many in those months of truce, in a much more universal sense than one dares to think today. 'There is always war,' replied Mordo Nahum memorably.

It is common knowledge that nobody is born with a decalogue already formed, but that everyone builds his own either during his life or at the end, on the basis of his own experiences, or of those of others which can be assimilated to his own; so that everybody's moral universe, suitably interpreted, comes to be identified with the sum of his former experiences, and so represents an abridged form of his biography. The biography of my Greek was linear; it was that of a strong and cold man, solitary and logical, who had acted from his infancy within the rigid framework of a mercantile society. He was also (or had been) open to other claims; he was not indifferent to the sky and the sea of his own country, to the pleasures of the home and of the family, to dialectical encounters; but he had been conditioned to drive all this back to the margins of his day and life, so that it would not disturb what he called the 'travail d'homme'. His life had been one of war, and he considered anyone who refused this iron universe of his to be despicable and blind. The Lager had happened to both of us; I had felt it as a monstrous upheaval, a loathsome anomaly in my history and in the history of the world; he, as a sad confirmation of things well known. 'There is always war,' man is wolf to man: an old story. He never spoke to me of his two years of Auschwitz.

He spoke to me instead, with eloquence, of his multiple

activities in Salonica, of goods bought, sold, smuggled by sea, or across the Bulgarian frontier by night; of frauds shamefully endured and of others gloriously perpetrated; and finally, of the happy and serene hours spent after the day's work by the shores of his bay, with his merchant colleagues, in cafés built on piles which he described to me with unusual freedom, and of the long discussions that took place there. What discussions? Of money, customs, freight charges, naturally, but of other things as well. What is the meaning of 'knowledge', 'spirit', 'justice', 'truth'. What is the nature of the slender tie that binds the soul to the body, how is it established at birth and dissolved at death. What is liberty, and how can one reconcile the conflict between the liberty of the spirit and fate. What follows death; and other great Greek matters. But naturally, all this in the evening, when business was over, with coffee or wine or olives, a lucid intellectual game between men active even in idleness; without passion.

Why the Greek recounted these matters to me, why he confessed to me, is not clear. Perhaps in front of me, so different, so foreign, he still felt alone, and his discourse was a monologue.

We left the kitchen in the evening, and returned to the Italians' barracks; after much insistence, we had gained permission from the Italian colonel, the head of the camp, to stay in the barracks one more night – but only one. No food, and we were not to show ourselves too much, he did not want trouble with the Russians. The morning after we should have to leave. We dined on two eggs apiece, from those purchased in the morning, keeping the last two for breakfast. After the events of the day, I felt myself very 'junior' compared to the Greek. When we came to the eggs, I asked him if he knew how to distinguish a raw egg from a hard-boiled one from the outside. (One spins the egg rapidly, for example on a table; if it is hard boiled it spins for a long time, if it is raw it stops almost at once); it was a little trick I was proud of, I hoped the Greek did not know it, and that I could thus rehabilitate myself in his eyes, at least in small measure.

But the Greek stared at me coldly, like a wise serpent: 'What do you take me for? Do you think I was born yesterday? Do you think I have never dealt in eggs? Come on, tell me an article I have never dealt in!'

I had to beat a retreat. The episode, negligible in itself, came back to me many months later, in the height of summer in the heart of White Russia, on the occasion of what was to be my third and last meeting with Mordo Nahum.

We left the following morning, at dawn (this is a story interwoven with freezing dawns), aiming at Katowice: we had received confirmation that various assembly centres really existed there for dispersed Italians, French, Greeks, etc. Katowice was only about fifty miles from Cracow, little more than an hour by train in normal times. But in those days one could hardly travel a dozen miles without changing trains, many bridges had been blown up, and because of the bad state of the lines the trains travelled with extreme slowness by day, and not at all by night. It was a labyrinthine journey, which lasted three days, with nocturnal halts in places ridiculously far from the straight line between the two extremes; a journey of cold and hunger. which took us on the first day to a place called Trzebinia. Here the train stopped, and I climbed down on the platform to stretch my legs, rigid from the cold. Perhaps I was among the first dressed in 'zebra' clothes to appear in that place called Trzebinia; I immediately found myself the centre of a dense group of curious people, who interrogated me volubly in Polish. I replied as best I could in German; and in the middle of the group of workers and peasants a bourgeois appeared, with a felt hat, glasses and a leather briefcase in his hand – a lawyer.

He was Polish, he spoke French and German well, he was

an extremely courteous and benevolent person; in short, he possessed all the requisites enabling me finally, after the long year of slavery and silence, to recognize in him the messenger, the spokesman of the civilized world, the first that I had met.

I had a torrent of urgent things to tell the civilized world: my things, but everyone's, things of blood, things which (it seemed to me) ought to shake every conscience to its very foundations. In truth, the lawyer was courteous and benevolent: he questioned me, and I spoke at dizzy speed of those so recent experiences of mine, of Auschwitz nearby, yet, it seemed, unknown to all, of the hecatomb from which I alone had escaped, of everything. The lawyer translated into Polish for the public. Now I do not know Polish, but I know how one says 'Jew' and how one says 'political'; and I soon realized that the translation of my account, although sympathetic, was not faithful to it. The lawyer described me to the public not as an Italian Jew, but as an Italian political prisoner.

I asked him why, amazed and almost offended. He replied, embarrassed: '*C'est mieux pour vous. La guerre n'est pas finie.*' The words of the Greek.

I felt my sense of freedom, my sense of being a man among men, of being alive, like a warm tide ebb from me. I found myself suddenly old, lifeless, tired beyond human measure; the war was not over, there was always war. My listeners began to steal away; they must have understood. I had dreamed, we had all dreamed, of something like this, in the nights at Auschwitz: of speaking and not being listened to, of finding liberty and remaining alone. After a while I remained alone with the lawyer; a few minutes later he also left me, urbanely excusing himself. He warned me, as the priest had done, against speaking German; when I asked for an explanation, he replied vaguely: 'Poland is a sad country.' He wished me good luck, he offered me money which I refused; he seemed to me deeply moved.

The locomotive was whistling its imminent departure. I climbed on the goods truck again, where the Greek was waiting for me, but I did not tell him of the episode.

This was not the only halt; others followed, and in one of them, in the evening, we realized that Szczakowa, the place with hot soup for everybody, was not far away. It was in fact to the north, and we had to go west, but as there was hot soup for everybody at Szczakowa, and we had no other programme except to satisfy our hunger, why not aim at Szczakowa? So we got down, waited until a suitable train passed, and presented ourselves again and again at the Red Cross counter; I think that the Polish sisters recognized me easily, and that they still remember me today.

When night came, we prepared to sleep on the floor in the middle of the waiting-room, as all the places by the walls were already taken. Some hours later a Polish policeman arrived, moustached, ruddy and corpulent. Perhaps out of pity or perhaps out of curiosity about my dress, he interrogated me in vain in Polish; I replied with the first phrase that one learns in every foreign language, and that is, '*nye rozumyen po polsku*', I do not understand Polish. I added, in German, that I was Italian and that I spoke a little German. At which, miracle! the policeman began to speak Italian.

He spoke a terrible Italian, guttural and aspirated, interwoven with portentous oaths unknown to me. He had learnt it, and this explained everything, in a valley of northern Italy, where he had worked for some years as a miner. He too, and he was the third, warned me not to speak German. I asked him why; he replied with an eloquent gesture, passing his index and middle fingers, like a knife, between his chin and larynx, and adding very cheerfully: 'Tonight all Germans kaputt.'

It was undoubtedly an exaggeration, or at any rate wishful thinking; but in fact the next day we passed a long train of cattle-trucks, closed from the outside; they were going east, and from the slits one could see many human mouths gaping for air. This spectacle, strongly evocative, aroused in me a mixture of confused and contradictory feelings, which even today I have difficulty in disentangling.

The policeman, with great kindness, proposed that the Greek and myself spend the rest of the night in warmth, in the jail; we accepted willingly, and only woke up in the unusual surroundings late in the morning, after a refreshing sleep.

We left Szczakowa the day after, for the last lap of our journey. We reached Katowice without trouble, where there really existed an assembly camp for Italians, and another for Greeks. We left each other without many words: but at the moment of farewell, in a fleeting but distinct manner, I felt a solitary wave of friendliness towards my Greek, streaked with tenuous gratitude, contempt, respect, animosity, curiosity and regret that I should not see him again.

I was in fact to see him again – twice. I saw him in May, in the glorious and turbulent days at the end of the war, when all the Greeks of Katowice, about a hundred men and women, passed singing in front of our camp, as they marched towards the station; they were going back to their country, to their homes. At the head of the column was he, Mordo Nahum, a lord among the Greeks, and it was he who bore the blue and white standard; but he put it down when he saw me, came out of the ranks to salute me (a little ironically, for he was leaving and I was staying; but it was just, he explained to me, because Greece belonged to the United Nations), and with an unaccustomed gesture took a gift out of his famous sack: a pair of trousers, of the type used in Auschwitz in the last months, that is with a large 'window' on the left hip, closed by a patch of striped cloth. Then he disappeared.

But he was to appear once more, many months later, against the most improbable of backgrounds and in the most unexpected of incarnations.

4. Katowice

THE TRANSIT CAMP of Katowice, which welcomed me hungry and tired after the week of wanderings with the Greek, was situated on a low hill in a suburb of the city called Bogucice. Formerly it had been a small German Lager, and had housed the miner-slaves working in a nearby coalpit. It consisted of a dozen brick huts, of small dimensions, and a single storey; there still existed the double barbed wire enclosure, now purely symbolic. The entrance was guarded by a solitary Soviet soldier, of a somnolent and idle mien; on the opposite side there was a large hole in the enclosure, through which one could leave without even bending down: the Russian Command did not seem to worry about it at all. The kitchens, canteen, infirmary and washrooms were outside the enclosure, so that the entrance was subject to a continual traffic.

The guard was a huge Mongolian, about fifty years old, armed with a sten-gun and bayonet, with enormous knobbly hands, grey drooping Stalin-type moustaches and fiery eyes; but his ferocious and barbaric appearance was wholly inconsistent with his innocent duties. He was never relieved, and so died of boredom. His behaviour towards those who used the entrance was unforeseeable; sometimes he demanded your *propusk*, that is, your permit; at other times he only asked your name; at other times again a little tobacco, or nothing at all. On certain other days, however, he ferociously repulsed everybody, but did not mind if he then saw them leaving by the hole at the back of the camp, even though it was plainly visible. When it was cold, he simply left his post, entered one of the dormitories where he saw a chimney smoking, threw his sten-gun on a bunk, lit his pipe, offered vodka if he had some, or asked for it if he had none, and swore despondently if no-one gave him any. Sometimes he even gave his sten-gun to the first of us he came across, and by gestures and shouts made him understand that he was to act as substitute at the guard-post; then he dozed off near the stove.

When I arrived there with Mordo Nahum, the camp was occupied by an extremely promiscuous population of about four hundred. There were French, Italians, Dutch, Greeks, Czechs, Hungarians and others; some had been civilian workers of the Todt Organization, others military internees, still others ex-Häftlinge. There were also about a hundred women.

In practice, the organization of the camp was really left to individual or group initiative; but nominally the camp was under a Soviet Kommandantur which was the most picturesque example of a gypsy encampment that one could imagine. There was a captain, Ivan Antonovich Egorov, a little man, no longer young, with a rustic and repulsive air; three lieutenants; a sergeant, athletic and jovial; a dozen territorial-army soldiers (including the guard with moustaches described above); a quartermaster; a *doktorka*; a medical doctor, Pyotr Grigoryevich Danchenko, extremely young, a great drinker, smoker, lover, a negligent person; a nurse, Marya Fyodorovna Prima, who soon became my friend; and an indefinite flock of girls as solid as oaks; nobody knew if they were military personnel or mobilized or auxiliaries or civilians or dilettanti. This last group had various and vague duties; washer-women, cooks, typists, secretaries, waitresses, lovers *pro tem.* of one or another man, intermittent fiancées, wives, daughters.

The whole troupe lived in harmony, without timetable or regulations, near the camp, lodged in the buildings of an abandoned primary school. The only person to take care of us was the quartermaster, who seemed to be the highest in authority, although not in rank, of the whole Command. In any case, their entire hierarchical relationships were indecipherable; for the most part, they lived together with friendly simplicity, like a large temporary family, without military formalism; sometimes furious quarrels and fights broke out, even between officers and soldiers, but they ended quickly without disciplinary consequences or bitterness, as if nothing had happened.

The war was about to finish, the long war that had devastated their country; for them it was already over. It was the great truce; for the other harsh season which was to follow had not yet begun, nor as yet had the ill-omened name of Cold War been pronounced. They were cheerful, sad and tired, and took pleasure in food and wine, like Ulysses' companions after the ships had been pulled ashore. And yet, under their slovenly and anarchical appearance, it was easy to see in them, in each of those rough and open faces, the good soldiers of the Red Army, the valiant men of the old and new Russia, gentle in peace and fierce in war, strong from an inner discipline born from concord, from reciprocal love and from love of their country; a stronger discipline, because it came from the spirit, than the mechanical and servile discipline of the Germans. It was easy to understand, living among them, why this former discipline, and not the latter, had finally triumphed.

One of the buildings in the camp was inhabited by Italians only, almost all civilian workers, who had gone to Germany more or less voluntarily. They were builders and miners, no longer young, quiet folk, sober, laborious, of gentle spirit.

But the camp leader of the Italians, to whom I was directed to be 'enlisted', was very different. Accountant Rovi had become camp leader not by election from below, nor by Russian investiture, but by self-nomination; in fact, although he was an individual of somewhat meagre intellectual and moral qualities, he possessed to a notable degree that virtue which under any sky is the most necessary to win power – the love of power for its own sake.

To watch the behaviour of a man who acts not according to reason, but according to his own deep impulses, is a spectacle of extreme interest, similar to that which the naturalist enjoys when he studies the activities of an animal of complex instincts. Rovi had achieved his office by acting with the same atavistic spontaneity as a spider spinning its web; like the spider without its web, so Rovi did not know how to live without his office. He had begun to spin immediately; he was basically foolish, and did not know a word of German or Russian, but from the first day he had secured for himself the services of an interpreter, and had presented himself in a ceremonial manner to the Soviet Command as plenipotentiary for Italian interests. He had organized a desk, with official forms (in beautiful handwriting with flourishes), rubber stamps, variously coloured pencils and a ledger; although he was not a colonel, in fact not even a soldier, he had hung outside his door an ostentatious placard 'Italian Command – Colonel Rovi'; he had surrounded himself with a small court of scullions, scribes, acolytes, spies, messengers and bullies, whom he paid in kind, with food taken from the rations of the community, and with exemption from all jobs of common interest. His courtiers, who, as always happens, were far worse than he, ensured (even by force, which was rarely necessary) that his orders were carried out, served him, gathered information for him, and flattered him intensely.

With surprising foresight, which is another way of saying by a highly complex and mysterious mental process, he had understood the importance, in fact the necessity, of owning a uniform, given that he had to deal with people in uniform. He had created quite a theatrical one, not without fantasy, out of a pair of Soviet boots, a Polish railwayman's cap and a jacket and pair of trousers found heaven knows where, which seemed to have belonged to a Fascist uniform and perhaps had; he had had badges sewn on the collar, gold braid on the cap, stripes and chevrons on the sleeves, and had covered his chest with medals.

However, he was not a tyrant, and not even a bad administrator. He had the good sense to keep molestations, extortions and abuses of authority within modest limits, and possessed an undeniable vocation for red tape. Now, since these Russians were curiously sensitive to the fascination of red tape (of which however they wholly missed the ultimate rational significance), and since, it seemed, they loved bureaucracy with that platonic and spiritual love which does not arrive at or desire possession, Rovi was benevolently tolerated, albeit not really appreciated, in the environment of the Kommandantur. Furthermore, he was bound to Captain Egorov by a paradoxical impossible tie of sympathy between misanthropes; for both were sad individuals, afflicted, disgusted and dyspeptic, and sought isolation in the general euphoria.

In the camp of Bogucice I found Leonardo, already accredited as a doctor, and besieged by a scarcely profitable but extremely numerous clientele; like myself he had come from Buna, and had arrived at Katowice a few weeks earlier, following less intricate paths than mine. Among the Häftlinge of Buna there were far too many doctors, and few (in practice, only those who spoke German, or who were extremely skilled in the art of survival) succeeded in gaining recognition as such by the head doctor of the S.S. So Leonardo had not enjoyed any privileges; he had been subjected to the most wearing manual tasks, and had lived his year of Lager in an extremely precarious manner. He painfully endured the fatigue and the cold, and had been sent to the infirmary countless times, for oedema of the feet, infected wounds and general undernourishment. Three times, in three infirmary selections, he had been chosen to die in the gas chamber, and three times he had narrowly escaped his fate through the solidarity of his colleagues in office. However, besides good fortune, he also possessed another virtue essential for those places: an unlimited capacity for endurance, a silent courage, not innate, not religious, not transcendent, but deliberate and willed hour by hour, a virile patience, which sustained him miraculously to the very edge of collapse.

The infirmary of Bogucice was to be found in the same school which lodged the Russian Command, in two small, quite clean rooms. It had been created from nothing by Marya Fyodorovna: Marya was a military nurse of about forty, with oblique and wild eyes, short nose with flared nostrils, and the agile, silent movements of a forest cat. In fact, she came from the forests; she was born in the heart of Siberia.

Marya was an energetic, stormy, disorderly and brisk woman. She procured drugs, partly through the normal administrative channels, drawing on the Soviet military depots; partly through the multiple channels of the black market; and partly (and it was the major part) by co-operating actively in sacking the warehouses of the former German Lagers and the abandoned German infirmaries and pharmacies, whose reserves had previously been the fruit of sacks carried out by the Germans among all the nations of Europe. So every day supplies arrived at the infirmary of Bogucice without plan or method: hundreds of boxes of pharmaceutical specialities, with labels and instructions in every language, which needed to be ordered and catalogued for possible use.

One of the most important things I had learnt in Auschwitz was that one must always avoid being a nobody. All roads are closed to a person who appears useless, all are open to a person who has a function, even the most fatuous. So after I had taken counsel with Leonardo, I presented myself to Marya, and offered my services as a polyglot-pharmacist.

Marya Fyodorovna examined me with an eye expert in weighing up males. Was I a '*doktor*'? Yes, I was, I maintained, assisted in my ambiguity by the strong linguistic discord; the Siberian woman, in fact, did not speak German, but (although she was not Jewish) she knew a little Yiddish, learnt heaven knows where. I did not have a very professional or a very attractive air, but perhaps I was passable for work in a back room: Marya took a crumpled piece of paper out of her pocket, and asked me what was my name.

When I added 'Primo' to 'Levi', her green eyes lit up, at first suspectingly, then inquiringly, finally benevolently. But then we were almost relations, she explained to me. I 'Primo' and she 'Prima'; 'Prima' was her surname, her '*familia*', Marya Fyodorovna Prima. Excellent, I could have the job. Shoes and clothes? Well, it was no easy matter, she would speak about it to Egorov and to some of her acquaintances, perhaps something could be found later. She scribbled my name on the piece of paper and the following day solemnly gave me the *propusk*, a permit of a somewhat homely appearance, which authorized me to enter and leave the camp at any hour of the day or night.

I lived in a room with eight Italian workers, and every morning I went to the infirmary to work. Marya Fyodorovna passed on to me many hundreds of coloured boxes to classify, and gave me small friendly presents: boxes of glucose (extremely welcome), liquorice and mint tablets; shoelaces; sometimes a packet of salt or custard powder. One evening she invited me for tea in her room, and I noticed that on the wall above her bed hung seven or eight photographs of men in uniform; they were almost all portraits of well-known faces, of the soldiers and officers of the Kommandantur. Marya called them all familiarly by name and spoke of them with affectionate simplicity; she had known them for so many years now, and they had fought the whole war together.

63

After a few days, as my work as pharmacist left me with a lot of free time, Leonardo called me to help him in the surgery. The Russian intention had been to restrict the surgery to the members of the Bogucice camp; in fact, as the treatment was free and without any formalities, Russian soldiers, civilians from Katowice, people passing through, beggars and doubtful figures who did not want to have anything to do with the authorities also came to ask for examination or medicines.

Neither Marya nor Doctor Danchenko had anything to say about this state of affairs (not that Danchenko ever had anything to say about anything; nor did he concern himself about anything except courting the girls, which he did with the mannerisms of an operetta grand duke; early in the morning, when he came for a rapid inspection, he was already drunk and full of happiness). Nevertheless, a few weeks later, Marya summoned me, and with a very official air informed me that 'by order of Moscow' the activities of the surgery had to be subjected to a minute control. So I would have to keep a register, and each evening note down the name and age of the patients, their illness, and the type and quantity of medicines provided or prescribed.

In itself, the matter did not seem without sense; but it was necessary to clarify certain practical details, which I discussed with Marya. For example, how could we be sure of the identity of the patients? But Marya thought the objection trifling; 'Moscow' would certainly be satisfied if I wrote down the general particulars as declared. But a more serious difficulty arose; in what language was the register to be kept? Not in Italian or French or German, which neither Marya nor Danchenko knew. In Russian? No, I did not know Russian. Marya meditated, perplexed, then she brightened up, and exclaimed: 'Galina!' Galina would save the situation.

Galina was one of the girls attached to the Kommandantur; she knew German, so I could dictate the minutes to her in

German, and she could translate them into Russian on the spot. Marya immediately sent for Galina (Marya's authority, although ill-defined, seemed great), and so began our collaboration.

Galina was eighteen, and came from Kazàtin in the Ukraine. She was dark, cheerful and graceful; she had an intelligent face with sensitive, petite features, and was the only one of her group to dress with a certain elegance, and the only one with shoulders, hands and feet of acceptable dimensions. She spoke German reasonably; with her help the famous minutes were laboriously manufactured evening by evening, with the stub of a pencil, on a block of greyish paper that Marya had handed to me like a holy relic. How does one say 'asthma' in German? And 'ankle'? And 'sprain'? And what are the corresponding Russian terms? At every linguistic obstacle we were forced to stop full of doubt and to fall back on complicated gestures, which ended in peals of laughter from Galina.

Far more rarely from me. Face to face with Galina I felt weak, ill and dirty; I was painfully conscious of my miserable appearance, of my badly shaved face, of my Auschwitz clothes; I was acutely conscious of Galina's glance, still almost infantile, in which vague compassion was mixed with definite repulsion.

Nevertheless, after a few weeks of working together, an atmosphere of tenuous reciprocal confidence had settled between us. Galina gave me to understand that the business of the minutes was not all that serious, that Marya Fyodorovna was 'old and mad' and would be satisfied so long as the sheets she received were covered with writing, and that Doctor Danchenko was busy in wholly other matters (known to Galina in amazing detail) with Anna, with Tanya, with Vassilissa, and that he was as interested in the minutes as in 'last year's snow'. So the time dedicated to the melancholic bureaucratic gods began to dwindle, and Galina profited from the intervals to tell me her story in bits and pieces, while smoking distractedly.

In the middle of the war, two years previously, she had been conscripted by this very Kommandantur in the Caucasus where she had taken refuge with her family; conscripted in the simplest of ways, that is stopped on the road, and taken to the Command H.Q. to type a few letters. She had gone there and she had stayed; she had been unable to detach herself (or more probably, I thought, she had not even tried). The Kommandantur had become her real family; she had followed it for thousands of miles, along the dislocated supply lines and interminable front, from the Crimea to Finland. She did not have a uniform, or even a specific post or rank, but she was useful to her fighting companions, she was their friend, and so she followed them, because there was the war, and everyone had to do his duty; moreover, the world was large and varied, and it was fun to wander around when one was young and without worries.

Galina had not even the shade of a worry. One met her in the morning going to the laundry with a bundle of washing balanced on her head, singing like a thrush; or in the offices of the Command H.Q. barefooted, hammering away at a typewriter; or on Sundays walking along the boulevard, arm in arm with a soldier, never the same one; or in the evening on the balcony, romantically entranced, while a smitten Belgian, in rags, serenaded her on the guitar. She was a country girl, alert, ingenuous, a bit of a flirt, very vivacious, not particularly well educated, or particularly serious; yet one felt in her the same force, the same dignity as in her comrades and boyfriends, the dignity of a man who works and knows why, of a man who fights and knows that he is in the right, of a man who has his life ahead of him.

In the middle of May, a few days after the end of the war, she came to say good-bye to me. She was leaving: they had told her she could go home. Did she have her travel-warrant?

Did she have her train fare? 'No,' she replied smiling, '*Nye nada*,' there was no need, in these matters one always found a way out; and she disappeared, sucked up into the emptiness of Russian space, along the paths of her endless country, leaving behind her a sharp scent of earth, of youth and of joy.

I also had other duties; to help Leonardo in the surgery, naturally; and to help Leonardo in the daily check for lice.

This last service was necessary in those countries and in those times, when petechial typhus crept about, endemic and mortal. The job was not very attractive; we had to go through all the huts, and ask everybody to strip to the waist and hand us his shirt, in whose creases and seams the lice normally nestled and laid eggs. This type of louse has a red spot on its back; according to a pleasantry which was repeated endlessly by our patients, if the spot was sufficiently enlarged a minute hammer and sickle would be seen. Lice are also called 'the infantry', with fleas as the artillery, mosquitoes as the air force, bugs as the parachutists, and crab-lice as the sappers. In Russia they are called *vshi*; I learnt that from Marya, who had given me a second block of paper on which to note the number and name of those with lice each day, and to underline the backsliders in red.

The backsliders were rare, with the single notable exception of Ferrari. Ferrari was a prodigy of inertia. He belonged to a small group of ordinary criminals, formerly held at San Vittore, the main prison at Milan, to whom the Germans had given the option in 1944 of imprisonment in Italy or labour service in Germany, and who had opted for the latter. There were about forty, almost all thieves or receivers; they formed a closed colourful and turbulent microcosm, a perpetual source of trouble for the Russian Command and for Mr Rovi.

But Ferrari was treated by his colleagues with open contempt, and so found himself relegated to an obligatory solitude. He was a small man, about forty, thin and sallow, almost bald, with an absent-minded expression. He spent his days stretched out on his bunk, and was an indefatigable reader. He read everything that came to hand: Italian, French, German, Polish newspapers and books. Every two or three days, at the moment of the check, he told me: 'I've finished that book. Have you another one to lend me? But not in Russian: you know that I have difficulty with Russian.' Not that he was a polyglot: in fact, he was practically illiterate. But he still 'read' every book, from the first line to the last, identifying the individual letters with satisfaction, pronouncing them with his lips, and laboriously reconstructing the words without bothering about their meaning. That was enough for him as, on different levels, others take pleasure in solving crossword puzzles, or integrating differential equations, or calculating the orbits of the asteroids.

He was a singular individual, as was confirmed by his story, which he willingly told me, and which I narrate here.

'For many years I attended the school for thieves at Loreto. There was this dummy fixed up with bells and a wallet in its pocket; one had to filch the wallet without the bells sounding, and I never succeeded. So they never authorized me to steal; they made me a guard. I was a guard for two years. The earnings are small and it's risky; it's not a good job.

'Chewing over this, one fine day I decided that, with or without authorization, if I wanted to earn my living I would have to set up on my own.

'There was the war, the evacuation, the black market, a crowd of people on the trams. I was on a Number Two tram, at Porta Ludovica, as no-one knew me in that area. Near me there was a woman with a large bag; in her coat pocket I could feel a wallet. I took out my *saccagno* very slowly and began to cut the pocket.'

I must open a brief technical parenthesis. The *saccagno*, Ferrari explained to me, is a precision instrument which is made by breaking in two the blade of an open razor. Its purpose is to cut bags and pockets, so it must be extremely sharp. Occasionally it is also used to disfigure people, in questions of honour; and this is why disfigured people are also called *saccagnati*.

'I had almost finished, when a woman, not the one with the pocket, mark you, but another, began to cry "Thief, thief!" I was doing nothing to her, she did not know me, and she didn't even know the woman with the pocket. She was not even from the police, she was somebody who had nothing to do with the matter at all. At any rate, the tram stopped, they caught me, I ended in San Vittore, and from there in Germany, and from Germany here. You see? That's what can happen if you're too enterprising.'

Since then, Ferrari had not been at all enterprising. He was the most submissive and docile of my patients; he undressed immediately without protest, handed me his shirt with the inevitable lice, and the morning after submitted to the disinfection without putting on airs like an offended lord. But the following day, the lice, heaven knows how, were there again. He was like that; he was no longer enterprising, he no longer put up resistance, not even to the lice.

My professional activity brought at least two advantages: the *propusk* and better food.

Food in Bogucice camp, in fact, was not short; we were given the Russian military ration, which consisted of two pounds of bread, two plates of soup a day, a *kasha* (that is, a dish with meat, lard, millet or other vegetables), and Russian-style tea, diluted, abundant and sweet. But Leonardo and I had to repair the damage caused by a year of Lager; we were still subject to an uncontrollable hunger, for the most part psychological, and the ration was not enough for us.

Marya had authorized us to eat our midday meal at the infirmary. The infirmary kitchen was run by two Parisian *maquisardes*, working-class women no longer young, also survivors from the Lager, where they had lost their husbands; they were taciturn and mournful women, whose past and recent sufferings appeared to be mastered and kept within limits on their precociously aged faces by the sharp moral consciousness of political fighters.

One of them, Simone, served at our table. She ladled out the soup once, and a second time. Then she looked at me, almost with mistrust: '*Vous répétez, jeune homme?*' Timidly I nodded assent, ashamed of my bestial greed. Under Simone's severe look, I rarely dared to '*répéter*' a fourth time.

As for the *propusk*, it formed a sign of social distinction rather than a specific advantage; in fact, anybody could easily leave through the hole in the fence, and go to the city as free as a bird in the sky. This is what many of the thieves did, to exercise their art at Katowice or even farther afield; they did not come back, or else they came back to the camp after a few days, often giving different names, not that anybody cared.

However, the *propusk* allowed one to make for Katowice without the long walk through the mud surrounding the camp. As my strength and the good season returned, I too felt an increasingly lively temptation to leave for a cruise through the unknown city; what use was it to have been liberated, if we still had to spend our days in a frame of barbed wire? Moreover, the people of Katowice were friendly towards us, and we had free tickets for the trams and cinemas.

One evening I spoke of this to Cesare, and we decided on a general programme for the following days, which would combine utility with pleasure, that is to say business with vagabondage.

5. Cesare

I HAD GOT to know Cesare in the last days of the Lager, but he was then a different Cesare. After the Germans had abandoned the camp of Buna, the infectious patients' ward, where the two French and I had succeeded in surviving and in installing an appearance of civilization, represented an island of relative comfort; in the adjoining ward, that of the dysentery patients, death ruled unopposed.

Through the wooden wall, a few inches from my head, I heard Italian being spoken. One evening, mustering what little energy I still possessed, I decided to go and see who was still living on the other side. I walked through the dark and frozen corridor, opened the door, and found myself thrown headlong into a kingdom of horror.

There were about a hundred bunks; at least half were filled with corpses stiffened by the cold. Only two or three candles broke the darkness; the walls and ceilings were lost in the shadows, so that it seemed like penetrating an enormous cavern. There was no heating except for the infectious breath of the fifty living patients. Despite the cold, the stink of faeces and death was so intense as to choke my breath, and I had to do violence to my lungs to force them to inhale the foul air.

Yet about fifty men were still living. They lay huddled under their blankets; some were groaning or shouting, others climbing painfully down from the bunks to relieve themselves on the floor. They were calling out names, praying, swearing, begging for help in all the languages of Europe.

I dragged myself gropingly along one of the passages between the three-storey bunks, stumbling and swaying in the dark on the layer of frozen excrement. On hearing my steps, the cries redoubled; bony hands came out from under the blankets, grabbed hold of my clothes, touched me icily on the face, tried to block my path. At last I reached the dividing wall at the end of the passage, and found whom I was looking for. There were two Italians in a single bunk, clinging to each other to keep out the cold: Cesare and Marcello.

I knew Marcello well; he came from Cannaregio, the old ghetto of Venice; he had been at Fossoli with me and had crossed the Brenner in the wagon next to mine. He was healthy and strong, and up to the last weeks of the Lager had held out valiantly, resisting the hunger and fatigue; but the cold of the winter had broken him. He no longer spoke, and in the light of my match I could barely recognize him: a yellow face, black with beard, all nose and teeth; his eyes bright and dilated with fever, staring into emptiness. For him there was little to be done.

Cesare, on the other hand, I barely knew, for he had arrived at Buna from Birkenau only a few months before. He asked for water before food: water, because he had not drunk for four days, and his fever was burning him, and his dysentery emptying him. I brought him some, together with the remains of our soup; I did not know that in this way I was laying the basis of a long and singular friendship.

His recuperative capacities must have been extraordinary, for I found him in the camp of Bogucice two months later, not only restored, but little less than flourishing, and as lively as a grasshopper; and this, despite an additional adventure which had severely tested the natural qualities of his astuteness, strengthened in the hard school of the Lager.

After the arrival of the Russians, he had been placed among the patients in Auschwitz, and as his illness was not serious, and his constitution robust, he recovered quickly – in fact, a little too quickly. About the middle of March, the German army in flight had concentrated around Breslau, and had tried one last desperate counter-offensive in the direction of the Silesian mining zone. The Russians had been taken by surprise; perhaps overestimating the enemy's initiative, they hastened to prepare a defensive line. They needed a long anti-tank trench to close the valley of the Oder between Oppeln and Gleiwitz; manpower was short, the work colossal, the need urgent, and the Russians saw to it according to their custom in an extremely expeditious and summary manner.

One morning, about nine o'clock, armed Russians suddenly blocked some of the main streets of Katowice. In Katowice, and in all Poland, there was a shortage of men; the male population of working age had disappeared, prisoners in Germany and Russia, dispersed among the partisan bands, massacred in battle, in the bombardments, in the reprisals, in the Lagers, in the ghettos. Poland was a country in mourning, a country of old men and widows. At nine in the morning there were only women in the street; housewives with their bags or handcarts, searching for food and fuel in the shops and markets. The Russians lined them up in rows of four, bags and all, took them to the station and sent them to Gleiwitz.

Simultaneously, that is five or six days before I arrived there with the Greek, they had unexpectedly surrounded the camp of Bogucice; they shouted like cannibals and fired shots in the air to frighten anybody attempting to run away. Without much ado they silenced their peaceful colleagues of the Kommandantur, who had sought timidly to intervene, they entered the camp with their sten-guns at the ready, and made everybody come out of the huts.

Thus on the main square of the camp a sort of parodied version of the German selections took place. A considerably less bloody version, as it was a question of going to work and not to death; but to make up for this, a far more chaotic and impromptu one.

While some of the soldiers went through the dormitories to dislodge the shirkers and then chase after them in a mad race like a great game of hide and seek, others stood by the door and examined one by one the men and women who were gradually presented to them by their hunters, or who presented themselves spontaneously. The judgement whether '*bolnoy*' or '*zdorovy*' (ill or healthy) was pronounced collectively, by acclamation, not without noisy disputes in controversial cases. The '*bolnoy*' was sent back to his hut; the '*zdorovy*' was lined up in front of the barbed wire fence.

Cesare was among the first to understand the situation ('to make out the movement', as he used to say in his colourful jargon); he had behaved with praiseworthy perspicacity, and only just failed to escape scot-free; he had hidden in the wood-deposit, a place nobody had thought about, and had remained there to the end of the hunt, very quiet and still under the pile of logs which he had pulled over himself. And then, some fool, in search of refuge, had come to hide there, bringing a Russian chasing after him. Cesare had been taken and declared healthy, purely as a reprisal, for when he came out of the woodpile he looked like a crucified Christ, or rather a defective cripple, and would have made a stone weep: he was trembling all over, he forced himself to slobber, and walked bandy-legged, limping, dragging a leg, with squinting, demented eyes. All the same, they had put him in the row of healthy people; after a few seconds, with lightning change of tactics, he had taken to his heels and tried to re-enter the camp by the hole at the back. But he had been overtaken, had received a clout and a kick on the shins, and had accepted defeat.

The Russians had taken them beyond Gleiwitz on foot, more than twenty miles; there they had lodged them as best they could in stables and barns, and had given them a dog's life with precious little to eat, and sixteen hours a day with pick-axe and spade, in rain or sun, with a Russian always there, sten-gun at the ready; the men at the trench, and the women (those from the camp and the Polish women they had found in the streets) peeling potatoes, cooking and cleaning.

It was tough; but the insult needled Cesare more than the work and hunger. To be caught with his pants down – he: a man who had kept a stall at Porta Portese: all Trastevere would laugh at him. He had to redeem his reputation.

He worked for three days; on the fourth, he bartered his bread for two cigars. One of them he ate; the other, he soaked in water and held in his armpit all night. The next day he was ready to report sick; he had all the symptoms, a galloping fever, terrible colic, giddiness, vomiting. They put him to bed; he stayed there until the intoxication had worked itself out, then at night-time he slipped away like a wraith and returned to Bogucice by short stages, with his conscience clear. I managed to settle him in my room, and we remained inseparable until the return journey.

'Here we are again,' said Cesare, pulling on his trousers gloomily when, a few days after his return, the nocturnal quiet of the camp was dramatically broken. It was an explosion, it was the Last Trumpet; Russian soldiers were running up and down the corridors, knocking on the doors with their rifle butts, yelling excited and incomprehensible orders; shortly after, the general staff arrived, Marya in hair curlers, Egorov and Danchenko half dressed, followed by Mr Rovi, bewildered and sleepy but in full uniform. We had to get up and dress, immediately. Why? Had the Germans come back? Were they transferring us? Nobody knew anything.

We finally managed to capture Marya. No, the Germans had not broken the front, but the situation was still very serious. '*Inspektsiya*': that very morning a general was coming from Moscow to inspect the camp. The entire Kommandantur was filled with panic and despair, a *dies irae* state of mind.

Rovi's interpreter galloped from dormitory to dormitory, shouting orders and counter-orders. Brooms, dusters, buckets appeared; every one was mobilized, the heaps of rubbish had to disappear, the windows had to be cleaned, the floors swept, the door handles polished, the cobwebs dusted away. We all began to work, yawning and swearing. Two o'clock went by, three o'clock, four o'clock.

About dawn, one began to hear people speaking of '*ubornaya*': the camp latrine really presented a problem.

It was a brick building, placed in the middle of the camp, large, striking, impossible to hide or camouflage. For months, nobody had bothered about its cleanliness or upkeep; inside, the floor was covered by a layer of stagnant filth, so deep that we had fixed large stones and bricks in it, which we could jump along in precarious equilibrium. From the doors and the cracks in the walls the filthy liquid overflowed outside, crossed the camp in the form of a stinking stream and vanished downhill in the midst of the fields.

Captain Egorov, who was sweating blood and had completely lost his head, chose a work squad of ten of us to go and clean up the latrine with brooms and buckets of chloride. But a child would have realized that ten men, even if given the right equipment, and not just brooms, would have taken at least a week; and as for the chloride, all the perfumes of Arabia would not have sweetened the place.

Not infrequently, senseless decisions emerge from the clash of two necessities where it would have been wiser to leave the dilemma to solve itself. An hour later (when the whole camp was buzzing like a disturbed beehive) the work squad was recalled, and we saw all twelve of the Command's territorial army men arrive, with planks, nails, hammers and rolls of barbed wire. In a twinkling all the doors and windows of the scandalous latrine were closed, barred, sealed with thick planks and all the walls, up to the roof, were covered by an inextricable tangle of barbed wire. Decency had been saved;

76

the most diligent of inspectors quite literally could not have placed a foot inside.

Midday came, then evening, and still no sign of the general. The following morning there was already less talk about him, on the third day none at all; the Russians of the Kommandantur had returned to their habitual and benign negligence and botchery, two planks had been taken down from the back door of the latrine and everything had returned to the old routine.

However, an inspector did come, a few weeks later; he came to check the running of the camp, and especially of the kitchens; he was not a general, but a captain wearing an armlet with the slightly ominous letters NKVD. He came, and he must have found particular pleasure in his duties – or in the girls of the Kommandantur, or in the air of Upper Silesia, or in the vicinity of the Italian cooks, because he did not go away, but stayed to inspect the kitchens every day until June (when we left) without apparently performing any other useful activity.

The kitchen, run by a barbaric cook from Bergamo, and an indeterminate number of fat, greasy voluntary helpers, was situated immediately outside the fence, and consisted of a large hut, almost wholly occupied by the two huge cauldrons resting on cement kilns. To enter one climbed two steps; there was no door.

The inspector carried out his first inspection with great dignity and seriousness, jotting down notes. He was a Jew, about thirty years old, extremely tall and bony, with a fine ascetic Don Quixote-like face. But by the second day he had dug out a motor-cycle, from heaven knows where, and he fell so passionately in love with it that henceforth the two were never seen apart.

The ceremony of the inspection became a public spectacle, watched by the citizens of Katowice in ever-growing numbers. The inspector arrived at about eleven o'clock, like a hurricane;

77

he braked suddenly with a terrible squeal, and pivoting on the front wheel made the back of the motor-cycle skid through ninety degrees. Without stopping, he aimed at the kitchen with lowered head, like a charging bull; he mounted the two steps with fearful bumpings, performed two cramped figures of eight round the cauldrons, the throttle wide open, once more flew past the steps on his way down, gave the public a military salute with a radiant smile, bent over the handlebars and disappeared in a cloud of glaucous smoke and much backfiring.

The game went smoothly for some weeks; then one day neither motor-cycle nor captain were to be seen. The latter was in hospital, with a broken leg; the former was in the loving hands of a cenacle of Italian *aficionados*. But they soon reappeared; the captain had had a bracket fitted to the frame of the motor-cycle and held his plastered leg on it in a horizontal position. His face, noble in its pallor, was bright with ecstatic happiness; fitted up like this, he once more began his daily inspection with hardly less impetus.

Only when April came, when the last snows had melted and the mild sun had dried the Polish mud, did we begin to feel ourselves truly free. Cesare had already been to town on various occasions, and insisted that I accompany him on his expeditions; I finally decided to overcome my inertia, and we left together on a glorious spring day.

At Cesare's request, as the experiment interested him, we did not leave by the hole in the fence. I left first by the main gate; the sentry asked my name, then asked for my permit and I gave it him. He checked it; the name corresponded. I turned the corner, and passed the piece of cardboard to Cesare through the barbed wire. The sentry asked Cesare his name: Cesare replied 'Primo Levi'. He asked for the permit: the name corresponded again, and Cesare left in a wholly legal manner. Not that Cesare is much concerned about acting legally; but he likes a sense of style, gamesmanship, putting one over on the next man without making him suffer.

We had entered Katowice as cheerful as schoolboys on holiday, but our happy-go-lucky mood was continually jarred by the spectacle which confronted us. At every step we came across the traces of the fearful tragedy which had touched us but had miraculously spared us. Graves at every corner, mute and hasty graves, without a cross but with the Red Star, of Soviet soldiers killed in battle. In one of the city's parks there was an endless war cemetery with crosses and stars intermingled, almost all bearing the same date: the date of the street battle, or perhaps of the last German massacre. In the middle of the main street stood three or four German tanks, seemingly intact, transformed into trophies and monuments, the gun of one of the tanks still aiming at an enormous hole, half-way up the house in front: the monster had died in the throes of destruction. Ruins everywhere, concrete frames, scorched wooden joists, corrugated-iron huts, people in rags, with a wild and famished look. At the important crossings, there were road signs put up by the Russians, forming a curious contrast to the tidiness and prefabricated precision of the analogous German signs we had seen earlier, and of the American ones we were to see later; rough planks of unvarnished wood, with hand-written names painted on in tar, in uneven Cyrillic characters: Gleiwitz, Cracow, Czestochowa; or rather, since the name was too long, 'Czestoch' on one plank, and then 'owa' on another smaller plank nailed underneath.

And yet the town was still living, after the nightmare years of the Nazi occupation, and the hurricane of the passing of the front. Many shops and cafés were open; the free market actually proliferated; the trams, coal mines, schools, cinemas were all functioning.

Since, on that first day, we did not have a penny between

us, we satisfied ourselves with a reconnaissance. After a few hours of walking in the sharp air, our chronic hunger had once more become acute: 'Come with me,' said Cesare, 'we're going to have lunch.'

He took me to the market, to the part where the fruit stalls were. At the first stall, under the jaundiced eyes of the stall-holder, he took a strawberry, only one strawberry, but a large one; he chewed it very slowly, with the air of an expert, then shook his head: '*Nyedobre*,' he said severely. ('It's Polish,' he explained to me; 'it means it's no good.') He passed to the next stall and repeated the scene; and so on with all the stalls until the last one. 'Well? What are you waiting for?' he then said to me with cynical pride; 'if you are hungry, you only have to act like me.'

All the same, the strawberry technique was not enough for our hunger; Cesare had understood the situation: it was high time to dedicate ourselves seriously to business.

He explained his intentions to me: he was a friend of mine, and was not asking me for anything; if I wanted, I could come to the market with him, perhaps even help him and learn the business, but what he really needed was a professional partner, with a small initial capital and some experience. In fact, he had already found such a man, a certain Giacomantonio, a villainous-looking old acquaintance of his from San Lorenzo prison. The terms of the partnership were extremely simple: Giacomantonio would buy, he would sell, and they would divide the profits equally.

Buy what? Everything, he told me: anything that came along. Although Cesare was little more than twenty years old, he boasted of a remarkable trading experience, comparable to that of the Greek. But, once the superficial analogies were over, I soon realized that an abyss lay between him and the Greek. Cesare was full of human warmth, always, at every moment of his life, not just outside office hours like Mordo Nahum. For Cesare, 'work' was sometimes an unpleasant necessity, at other times an amusing opportunity to meet people, and not a frigid obsession, or a luciferesque affirmation of himself. One of them was free, the other was a slave to himself; one was miserly and reasonable, the other prodigal and fantastic. The Greek was a lone wolf, in an eternal war against all, old before his time, closed in the circle of his own joyless pride; Cesare was a child of the sun, everybody's friend; he knew no hatred or contempt, was as changeable as the sky, joyous, cunning and ingenuous, bold and cautious, very ignorant, very innocent and very civilized.

I did not want to enter the agreement with Giacomantonio, but I willingly accepted Cesare's invitation to accompany him sometimes to the market, as an apprentice, an interpreter and a porter. I accepted it not only out of friendship, and a desire to escape the boredom of the camp, but above all because to watch Cesare's enterprises, even the most modest and trivial ones, constituted a unique experience, a live and fortifying spectacle, which reconciled me to the world and once more lit in me that joy of living which Auschwitz had extinguished.

A virtue like Cesare's is good in itself, in an absolute sense; it is enough to confer nobility upon a man, to redeem his many other defects, to save his soul. But at the same time, and on a more practical level, it is of priceless value for someone intending to practise his trade on a public square: in fact, nobody was insensitive to Cesare's charm, neither the Russians of the Command, nor our motley comrades of the camp, nor the citizens of Katowice who frequented the market. Now it is equally clear from the hard laws of commerce that what is of advantage to the seller is of disadvantage to the purchaser and vice versa.

April was drawing to its close, and the sun was already warm and generous, when Cesare came to wait for me at the end of the surgery. His murderous-looking companion had carried out a series of brilliant coups: for a total of fifty zloty

he had bought a fountain pen which did not write, a chronometer, and a woollen shirt in quite good condition. Then this
man Giacomantonio, with the expert nose of a receiver, had
had the excellent idea of mounting guard at Katowice station
in order to wait for the Russian trains returning from
Germany: these soldiers, now demobilized and on their way
home, were the easiest dupes imaginable. They were in carefree holiday spirits, had plenty of booty, did not know the
local prices, and needed ready money.

Apart from any utilitarian aim, it was in any case worth
while passing a few hours at the station, merely to watch the
extraordinary spectacle of the Red Army returning home: a
spectacle as dramatic and solemn as a biblical migration, and
at the same time as rambling and colourful as the passage of a
circus. Endless strings of cattle-trucks, used as military transports, stopped at Katowice: they were fitted out to travel for
months, perhaps as far as the Pacific Ocean, and carried, all
mixed together, thousands of soldiers and civilians, men and
women, former Russian prisoners of the Germans, and fresh
German prisoners of the Russians, as well as goods, furniture,
cattle, dismantled industrial plant, food, war materials, scrap
metal. They were travelling villages: some trucks contained
what seemed to be a family nucleus, one or two double beds,
a wardrobe with mirrors, a stove, a radio, chairs and tables.
Electric wires ran haphazardly between one truck and another, originating in the first truck with a generator; they
served for the lighting system and at the same time for
hanging out the washing to dry (and to grow black with soot).
When the sliding doors were opened in the morning half-
dressed men and women appeared with large sleepy faces,
who looked out puzzled from the background of these
domestic settings, with little idea of which part of the world
they found themselves in; then they got down to wash in the
freezing water of the hydrants, and offered round tobacco
and sheets of *Pravda* to roll cigarettes.

So I left for the market with Cesare, who intended to sell the three objects described above, perhaps to the Russians themselves. By now the market had lost its primitive character of a fair of human miseries. Rationing had been abolished, or rather had fallen into disuse; the peasants' carts arrived from the rich surrounding countryside with tons of lard and cheese, eggs, chickens, sugar, fruit, butter: a garden of temptations, a cruel challenge to our obsessive hunger, and to our lack of means, an imperious incitement to procure money.

Cesare sold the pen at the first attempt, for twenty zloty, without bargaining. He had absolutely no need of an interpreter: he spoke only Italian, or to be precise Roman dialect, or to be still more precise Roman ghetto slang, studded with corrupt Hebrew words. Clearly he had no choice, because he did not know any other language; but, unknown to him, this ignorance played heavily in his favour. Cesare was playing on his home ground, to use sporting terms; on the other hand, his clients, intent on interpreting his incomprehensible speech and novel gestures, were distracted from the necessary concentration; if they made counter-offers, Cesare did not understand them, or stubbornly pretended not to understand them.

The art of the charlatan is not so widespread as I thought; the Polish public seemed to be unaware of it, and was fascinated. Moreover, Cesare was also a first-class mimic; he waved the shirt in the sun, holding it tightly by the collar (under the collar there was a hole, but Cesare held the shirt in his hand at the very place with the hole), and he declaimed its praises with torrential eloquence, with new and senseless additional digressions, suddenly addressing one or another member of the public with obscene nicknames which he invented on the spot. He stopped abruptly (he knew by instinct the oratorical value of pauses), kissed the shirt with affection, and then began again, with a resolute yet desolate

83

voice, as if it tore his heart to part with it, and he was only doing it for love of his neighbour: 'You, Big Belly,' he said, 'how much will you give me for this little *koshoola* of mine?'

The Big Belly was dumbfounded. He looked at 'the little koshoola' with desire, and glanced around out of the corner of his eye, half hoping and half fearing that someone else would make the first offer. Then he came forward hesitantly, held out an uncertain hand and mumbled something like '*pinjeeshi*'. Cesare clutched the shirt to his chest as if he had seen a snake. 'What did he say?' he asked me, as if he suspected that he had been mortally insulted; but it was a rhetorical question, for he recognized (or guessed) Polish numbers much more quickly than I.

'You're mad,' he then stated categorically, pointing his index finger at his temple and turning it like a drill. The public rumbled with laughter, visibly siding with this preposterous foreigner who had come from the ends of the earth to perform wonders in their market squares. The Big Belly stood agape rocking from foot to foot like a bear. '*Du fereek*,' continued Cesare pitilessly (he meant to say '*verrückt*'); then, to clarify, he added: '*du meschuge*.' A storm of savage laughter broke out; everyone had understood this. '*Meschuge*' is a Hebrew word which has survived in Yiddish, and as such is universally understood in all Central and Eastern Europe: it means 'mad', but it carries the additional idea of an empty, melancholic, doltish and lunar folly.

The Big Belly scratched his head and hitched up his trousers, full of embarrassment. '*Sto*,' he then said, trying to make peace: '*Sto zlotych*,' a hundred zloty.

The offer was interesting. Cesare, somewhat appeased, turned to Big Belly as man to man, with a persuasive voice, as if to convince him of some involuntary yet clumsy transgression of his. He spoke to him at length, opening up his heart, with warmth and confidence, explaining to him: 'You see? You understand? Don't you agree?'

'*Sto zlotych*,' repeated the other obstinately.

'He is a *testa dura*, as stubborn as a mule,' Cesare said to me. Then, as if overcome by unexpected tiredness, and in a final attempt to reach agreement, he put a hand on his shoulder and said to him maternally: 'Listen. Listen, pal. You haven't understood me. Let's try it this way. You give me this much' (and with his finger he traced 150 on his belly), 'you give me *Sto Pinjeeshi*, and it's all yours. Agreed?'

The Big Belly mumbled and shook his head negatively, staring at the ground; but Cesare's clinical eye had caught the sign of capitulation: an imperceptible movement of his hand towards the back pocket of his trousers.

'Come on. Shake out those shekels!' Cesare rushed on, striking while the iron was hot. The money was finally produced and the shirt changed hands. But immediately Cesare tore me from my ecstatic admiration.

'Come on, lad. Let's hop it, before he puts his hand through the hole.' So, fearful lest the client discover the hole too quickly, we hopped it, forgoing our attempt to get rid of the unsaleable chronometer. We walked at a slow dignified pace as far as the nearest corner, then we cut and ran as fast as our legs would carry us, and returned to the camp by devious routes.

6. Victory Day

LIFE IN THE camp of Bogucice, the surgery and the market, rudimentary human relations with Russians, Poles, and others, rapid oscillations between hunger and a full belly, between hopes of return and disappointment, expectancy and uncertainty, barrack life and improvisations, almost a spurious form of military life in a temporary and foreign environment, aroused in me discomfort, nostalgia and, above all, boredom. On the other hand it agreed with Cesare's habits, character and aspirations.

At Bogucice, Cesare flourished visibly, day by day, like a tree nourished by the spring sap. At the market he now had a fixed place and an affectionate clientele, created from nothing by himself by virtue of nicknames: The Bearded Lady, Skin and Bones, Booby, as many as three Buttocks, The Street Walker, Frankenstein, a Junoesque girl whom he called the Old Bailey, and many others. In the camp, he enjoyed unquestioned prestige: he had quarrelled with Giacomantonio, but many others entrusted him with goods to sell, without a contract, purely on trust, so that he was never short of money.

One evening he disappeared: he did not come back to camp for dinner, or to the dormitory to sleep. Naturally, we did not report anything to Rovi, still less to the Russians, so as not to create complications; nevertheless, when his absence had lasted for three days and nights, even I, who by nature am not very apprehensive, and was even less so as regards Cesare, began to feel slightly uneasy.

Cesare returned at dawn of the fourth day, as dishevelled and bristly as a cat returning from a roof-top jamboree. He had bags under his eyes, but they still shone with a proud light. 'Leave me alone,' he said as soon as he entered, although no-one had asked him anything, and most of us were still snoring. He threw himself on his bunk with an air of extreme exhaustion; but after a few minutes, unable to contain the great secret pent up inside him, he came over to me just as I was waking up. In a hoarse voice, with a grim expression on his face as if he had been at a witches' sabbath for the past three nights, he told me: 'I've made it at last. I've got a *panienca.*'

The news did not sound particularly thrilling to me. He was certainly not the first to manage it; other Italians, particularly soldiers, had got themselves a girl in the city; for '*panienca*' is the exact equivalent of '*segnorina*', with an equally distorted sound.*

It was not a very difficult undertaking, since men were scarce in Poland; in fact, many Italians had 'established' themselves, impelled not merely by the national amatory myth, but also because they felt a deeper and more serious need, a nostalgia for a home and for affection. As a result, the dead or distant husband had been replaced not only in the woman's heart and bed, but in some cases in all his duties: Italians could be seen going to work in the coalfields together with Poles in order to carry their wages 'home', or serving behind the counter in a store, while strange families were to be seen on Sundays, walking decorously along the boulevards, the Italian arm in arm with a Polish girl, holding an excessively blond child by the hand.

But, Cesare explained to me, his case was different (all cases are always different, I thought, yawning). His *panienca* was beautiful, unmarried, elegant, clean, in love with him, and therefore inexpensive. Besides this, she was extremely experienced; her only defect was that she spoke Polish. So if I were his friend, I had to help him.

* 'Segnorina', a distortion of 'Signorina' (young lady), became current in Italy to describe the Allied soldiers' girl-friends, near-prostitutes.

87

I was hardly in a position to help him very much, I wearily explained to him. In the first place, I did not know more than thirty words of Polish; in the second place, I was wholly lacking in the sentimental terminology he required; in the third place I did not feel in the right mood to go with him. But Cesare refused to give up: perhaps the girl understood German. He had in mind a very clear plan; so would I kindly stop being obstructive, and tell him the German for this, that and the other.

Cesare overestimated my linguistic knowledge. The things he wanted to learn from me are not taught in any German language course, nor had I had the slightest occasion to learn them in Auschwitz; moreover, they were such subtle and idiomatic questions that I suspect that they do not exist in any language other than Italian and French.

I explained my doubts to him, but Cesare looked offended. He put on his shoes and left, mumbling curses at me. I was being subversive, that was clear; it was sheer envy. He came back in the afternoon, and threw in front of me a nice pocket Italian-German dictionary which he had bought for twenty zloty at the market. 'There is everything here,' he told me with an air that admitted of no further discussion or quibbling. Alas, there was not everything; in fact the essential things were missing, those things which a mysterious convention expurgates from the universe of printed paper; it was money thrown away. Cesare went away again, disillusioned with culture, with friendship, indeed with printed paper itself.

From then on he paid only rare visits to the camp; his *panienca* provided generously for all his needs. At the end of April he disappeared for a whole week. Now, that was not the end of just any April; it was the memorable one of 1945.

Unfortunately we were not able to understand the Polish newspapers; but the size of the headlines which increased day by day, the names we could read on them, the very air we breathed in the streets and at the Kommandantur, made us understand that victory was near. We read 'Vienna', 'Koblenz', 'Rhine'; then 'Bologna'; then, with emotion and joy, 'Turin' and 'Milan'. Finally, 'Mussolini', in enormous letters, followed by an awesome and indecipherable past participle; and at last, in red ink, covering half a page, the final, cryptic and exhilarating announcement; 'BERLIN UPADL!'

On 30th April Leonardo, I and a few other passholders were summoned by Captain Egorov; with a curiously reserved and embarrassed air, which was untypical of him, he told us through the interpreter that we should have to hand back the *propusk*; the following day we should receive another one. Naturally we did not believe him, but we still had to give back the card. The measure seemed to us absurd and slightly annoying, and increased our anxiety and expectancy; but the next day we understood the reason.

For the next day was 1st May; it was followed on the 3rd by some important Polish holiday; on the 8th the war ended. The news, although expected, exploded like a hurricane; for eight days the camp, the Kommandantur, Bogucice, Katowice and the whole of Poland and the entire Red Army burst out in a fit of delirious enthusiasm. The Soviet Union is a gigantic country, and harbours within its heart gigantic vigour, a Homeric capacity for joy and abandon, a primordial vitality, an uncontaminated pagan appetite for carousals, carnivals, massive revelry.

In a few hours the atmosphere turned tropical. There were Russians everywhere, like ants coming out of an anthill; they embraced each other as if they were all old friends, and sang and shouted; although generally unsteady on their legs, they danced with each other, and overwhelmed anyone they happened to meet with embraces. They fired shots in the air, and sometimes not in the air; a young baby-faced soldier was brought to us in the surgery, a parachutist, with a bullet shot passing from his abdomen through his back. Miraculously the shot had not harmed any vital organs; the boy-soldier stayed in bed for three days and peacefully submitted to medical care, looking at us with eyes as virgin as the sea; then one evening, as a festive band of his companions passed by in the street, he jumped out of his bed fully dressed, wearing his uniform and boots, and like the good parachutist he was, simply threw himself into the road from the first-floor window before the eyes of the other patients.

The already tenuous traces of military discipline vanished. On the evening of 1st May the sentry snored drunken and sprawling on the ground in front of the camp gate, with his sten-gun on his shoulder; then he was seen no more. It was useless to go to the Kommandantur for anything urgent; the person responsible was not there, or was in bed sleeping off his drunkenness, or was engaged in mysterious and feverish preparations in the school gymnasium. It was extremely fortunate that the kitchen and surgery were in Italian hands.

What these preparations were for we soon found out. They were organizing a great party for Victory Day; a theatrical performance, with choruses, dancing and recitation, offered by the Russians to us, the guests of the camp. To us Italians; because in the meantime, as the other nationalities had been moved off according to some complicated plan, we had remained as a large majority at Bogucice, in fact, almost alone with a few French and Greeks.

Cesare came back to us on one of these tumultuous days. He was in an even worse condition than before; covered in mud from head to foot, in rags, haggard and suffering from a monstrously stiff neck. He had a bottle of Vodka in his hand brand new and full, and his first concern was to search around until he found another empty bottle; then, scowling and funereal, he created an ingenious funnel with a piece of cardboard, decanted the vodka, broke the bottle into small pieces, collected the fragments in a sheet of paper, and with an air of secrecy went to bury them in a hole at the back of the camp.

He had been struck by misfortune. One evening, returning from the market to the girl's house, he had found a Russian there; he had seen his military greatcoat in the hall with its belt and holster, and a bottle. He had taken the bottle, as a partial indemnity, and had wisely gone away; but the Russian had apparently come after him, perhaps because of the bottle, or perhaps through retrospective jealousy.

Here his account became more obscure and less plausible. He had sought in vain to escape and had soon convinced himself that the whole Red Army was on his tracks. He had ended up at a funfair, but even there the hunt had continued, throughout the night. He had spent the last few hours lurking under the floor of the dance hall, while all Poland danced on his head; but he had not abandoned the bottle, because it represented all that was left to him of a week of love. He had destroyed the original container as a precaution, and insisted that the contents be consumed immediately by his closest friends. It was a melancholic and taciturn drinking bout.

The 8th May came: a day of exultation for the Russians, of diffident vigil for the Poles, of joy tinged with deep nostalgia for us. From that day, in fact, our homes were no longer forbidden us, no war front now separated us from them, no concrete obstacle, only red tape; we felt that our repatriation was now our due, and every hour spent in exile weighed on us like lead; but the total lack of news from Italy weighed on us even more. Nevertheless, we all went to the Russians' show, and we did well.

The theatre had been improvised in the school gymnasium: in fact, everything had been improvised, actors, seats, choir, programme, lights, curtain. The tails worn by the compère, Captain Egorov in person, were strikingly improvised.

Egorov appeared on the stage blind drunk, fitted up with

an enormous pair of trousers which reached to his armpits, while his tails swept the floor. He was overcome by a desperate alcoholic despondency, and presented the various comic or patriotic numbers in the programme in a sepulchral voice, amid resounding sobs and fits of tears. His equilibrium was uncertain; at crucial moments he grabbed the microphone, and then the audience fell suddenly silent as when an acrobat leaps into space from his trapeze.

Everybody appeared on the stage: the whole Kommandantur. Marya directed the choir, which was excellent, as are all Russian choirs, and which sang *Moskva moya* ('My Moscow') with wonderful impetus and harmony and manifest good faith. Galina performed by herself, dressed in a Circassian costume and boots, in a giddy dance in which she revealed fantastic and unsuspected athletic talents; she was overwhelmed by applause, and thanked the audience with emotion, dropping innumerable eighteenth-century curtsies, her face as red as a tomato, and her eyes glittering with tears. Dr Danchenko and the Mongol with moustaches were as good: although full of vodka, they performed as a pair one of those demoniac Russian dances in which one jumps in the air, crouches down, kicks out and pirouettes on one's heels like a spinning top.

There followed a remarkable imitation of Charlie Chaplin, personified by one of the robust girls from the Kommandantur, with an exuberant bust and bottom, but punctiliously faithful to her prototype as regards bowler hat, moustache, shoes and cane. And finally, announced by Egorov in a tearful voice, and greeted by all the Russians with a savage shout of approval, there appeared on the stage Vanka Vstanka.

Who Vanka Vstanka is, I cannot really say: perhaps a character from a popular Russian mime. In this instance, he was a timid, dim-witted, love-lorn little shepherd, who wanted to declare his passion for his mistress but did not dare. His mistress was the huge Vassilissa, the Valkyrie responsible for the canteen, as dark as a raven, and muscular, capable of flooring at a swipe an unruly diner or an unfortunate wooer (more than one Italian had tried); but who would have recognized her on the stage? Here her rôle had transformed her; the guileless Vanka Vstanka (off stage one of the lieutenants), his face coated with white and pink powder, courted her from afar, in an Arcadian manner, through twenty melodious strophes unfortunately incomprehensible to us, stretching supplicating and hesitant arms towards his beloved; she repulsed him with smiling but resolute grace, warbling equally sweet and teasing replies. But slowly the distance diminished, while the noise of the applause increased in proportion; after much skirmishing, the two shepherds exchanged chaste kisses on the cheek, and ended by rubbing their backs against each other vigorously and sensuously to the irrepressible enthusiasm of the audience.

We left the theatre slightly dazed, but almost moved. The performance had satisfied our deepest feelings; it had been improvised in a few days, and this was noticeable; it was a home-made performance, unpretentious, puritanical, often childish. Yet it presupposed something not improvised, but deep-rooted and robust; a youthful intense native capacity for joy and self-expression, a loving and friendly familiarity with the stage and with the audience a long way removed from empty exhibitionism or intellectual abstractions, from conventionality or tired imitations. Consequently, within its limits, it had been a warm, alive performance, not vulgar, not commonplace, but generously free and self-assertive.

The following day everything had returned to normal and, except for slight shadows under their eyes, the Russians had resumed their habitual appearance. I met Marya at the surgery, and told her that I had greatly enjoyed myself, and that all the Italians had much admired her and her colleagues' theatrical qualities; it was the simple truth. Marya was, normally and by nature, a not very methodical but extremely practical woman, solidly rooted in the tangible immediacies of her everyday experience, friendly to men of flesh and hostile to the haze of theories. But how many human minds are capable of resisting the slow, fierce, incessant, imperceptible driving force of indoctrination?

She replied with didactic seriousness. She thanked me formally for the praise, and assured me that she would communicate it to the whole Command; then she informed me with great gravity that dancing and singing, as well as recitation, form part of the scholastic curriculum in the Soviet Union; that it is the good citizen's duty to perfect his abilities or natural talents; that the theatre is one of the most precious instruments of collective education; and other pedagogic platitudes, which sounded absurd and vaguely irritating to my ear, still full of the great gust of vitality and comic force of the previous evening.

On the other hand, Marya herself ('old and mad', according to the eighteen-year-old Galina's description) seemed to possess a second personality, quite distinct from her official one; for she had been seen the evening before, after the theatre, drinking like a fish, and dancing like a Bacchante until late at night, exhausting innumerable partners, like some possessed cavalier riding horse after horse into the ground.

Victory and peace were also celebrated in a different manner which, indirectly, almost cost me very dearly. In the middle of May a football match took place between the Katowice team and a team of Italians.

It was in fact a return game; a first match had been played without particular solemnity two or three weeks before, and had been won comfortably by the Italians against an anonymous and scratch team of Polish miners from the suburbs.

But for the return match the Poles took the field with a first-class team; word got about that some players, including the goalkeeper, had been brought for the occasion from no less a place than Warsaw, while the Italians, alas, were in no condition to do likewise.

The goalkeeper was a nightmare. He was a lamp-post of a man, blond, with an emaciated face, a concave chest, and slouching movements like an Apache. He had none of the leap, the emphatic crouch and the nervous twitching of the professional; he stood in the goal with insolent condescension, leaning against one of the posts as if he was only watching the game, with an outraged but also outrageous air. Yet the few times the ball was kicked at the goal by the Italians, he was always in its path, as if by chance, without ever making an abrupt movement; he would stretch out one – only one – long arm, which seemed to emerge from his body like a snail's horn and to possess the same invertebrate and adhesive quality. The ball stuck there solidly, drained of all its momentum; it slid down his chest, then down his body and leg, to the ground. He never used the other hand; during the whole match he kept it ostentatiously in his pocket.

The game was played on a ground in the suburbs at some distance from Bogucice and the Russians had given passes for the occasion to the entire camp. The match was fiercely disputed, not only between the rival teams, but also between both of these and the referee; for the referee, who was the guest of honour, the occupant of the V.I.P.s' box, the director of the match, and the linesman all at once, was the NKVD captain, the unsubstantial inspector of the kitchens. Now, with his fracture perfectly healed, he seemed to follow the game with intense interest, but not of a sporting kind; with an interest of a mysterious nature, perhaps aesthetic, perhaps metaphysical. His behaviour was irritating, in fact debilitating, if judged by the criteria of the many experts among the spectators; on the other hand, it was exhilarating, and worthy of a high-class clown.

He interrupted the game continually, arbitrarily, with piercing blasts of his whistle and with a sadistic preference for moments when the game was being fought at the goal's mouth; if the players did not listen to him (and they soon stopped listening to him, because the interruptions were so frequent), he leapt over the wall of his box with his long booted legs, threw himself into the mêlée whistling like a train, and would not let up until he had gained possession of the ball. Then sometimes, he would take it in his hand, turning it over and over with a suspicious air, as if it were an unexploded bomb; at other times, with imperious gestures, he would order it to be placed at a certain point on the field, then would go up to it, unsatisfied, and move it a few inches, walk around it thoughtfully for a long time and finally, as if convinced of heaven knows what, make a sign for the game to continue. At other times again, when he managed to get the ball at his feet, he would make everybody move away, and would kick it at the goal with all his strength; then he would turn radiantly to the public, which bellowed with anger, and salute it for a long time, clasping his hands above his head like a victorious boxer. He was, however, rigorously impartial.

In these conditions, the match (which was deservedly won by the Poles) dragged on for over two hours, until about six in the evening; probably it would have gone on until nightfall had it depended solely upon the captain, who was not in the least worried about the time, who behaved on the field as if he were the Lord's Anointed, and who seemed to derive a crazy and inexhaustible pleasure from his misinterpreted duties as director of the game. But as twilight came, the sky rapidly darkened, and when the first drops of rain fell he whistled the game to an end.

The rain soon turned into a deluge; Bogucice was far away, there was no shelter on the road, and we returned to the camp soaked to the skin. The next day I felt ill; my illness remained mysterious for a long time.

I could no longer breathe freely. It felt as though there

were a blockage somewhere in my lungs, an acute pain, a deep stabbing pang, which seemed to be located somewhere above my stomach, but behind, towards the back, and which impeded me from inhaling beyond a certain point. This point dropped, from day to day, from hour to hour; the ration of air it conceded me was reduced with a slow and constant progression that terrified me. On the third day I could no longer move; on the fourth, I lay on my bunk supine, immobile, with short frequent breaths like those of a panting dog.

7. The Dreamers

ALTHOUGH LEONARDO TRIED to hide it from me, he could
not understand, and was seriously worried by, my illness. It
was difficult to discover its real nature, because his entire
professional equipment consisted of one stethoscope; it
seemed not only difficult, but hardly advisable, to obtain permission from the Russians to send me to the civilian hospital
of Katowice; there was also little to be hoped for from Dr
Danchenko.

So for some days I remained stretched out, immobile,
drinking only a few spoonfuls of soup, for every time I tried
to move, or to swallow some solid food, the pain started up
savagely and cut short my breath. After a week of tortured
immobility, Leonardo, by dint of tapping my back and chest,
managed to discover a symptom: it was a dry pleurisy,
nestling insidiously between the two lungs, encumbering
the mediastinum and the diaphragm.

Then he did far more than is normally expected of a doctor.
He turned himself into a clandestine merchant and drug-
smuggler, sturdily assisted by Cesare, and walked miles
through the city, from one address to another, searching for
sulphonamides and calcium injections. He was not very
successful as regards the drugs, because sulphonamides were
extremely rare and could be found only on the black market
at prices which were prohibitive to us. But he found something better. He discovered a mysterious colleague in Katowice, who possessed a not very legal, but well-equipped,
surgery, a pharmaceutical stock, much money and free time,
and who was also Italian (or almost).

In fact, everything relating to Dr Gottlieb was wrapped up

in a thick cloud of mystery. He spoke Italian perfectly, but German, Polish, Hungarian and Russian equally well. He came from Fiume, Vienna, Zagreb and Auschwitz. He had been at Auschwitz, but he never stated in what quality or condition, nor was he a man to whom it was easy to put questions. It was difficult to understand how he had survived in Auschwitz, for he had an anchylosed arm; it was still more difficult to imagine by what secret paths, and in what fantastic manner he had managed to remain there, never separated from his brother and his equally mysterious brother-in-law, and then, within a few months of leaving the Lager, despite the Russians and the law, to become a wealthy man and the most esteemed doctor in Katowice.

He was a wonderfully equipped person. Intelligence and cunning emanated from him like energy from radium, with the same silent and penetrating continuity, without effort, without a pause, without a sign of exhaustion, in all directions at once. It was clear from the first that he was an excellent doctor. But I was never able to discover if his professional excellence was merely one aspect, one side of his high intellect, or if it was itself his instrument of penetration, his secret weapon to turn enemies into friends, to render prohibitions null, to change no into yes; this too formed part of the cloud in which he wrapped himself and which moved with him. It was an almost visible cloud, which made his looks and the lines of his face hard to decipher, and which led one to suspect, beneath every action of his, every phrase, every silence, the existence of a tactic and a technique, the pursuit of unperceivable ends, a continual shrewd labour of exploration, elaboration, penetration and possession.

Nevertheless, Dr Gottlieb's intelligence, aimed though it was at practical ends, was not inhuman. So abundant was his self-assurance, his expectancy of victory, his faith in himself, that a large portion remained to bestow on assisting his less gifted neighbours; and in particular on assisting us, for we had escaped like him from the mortal trap of the Lager, a circumstance about which he showed himself strangely sensitive.

Gottlieb restored my health like a thaumaturge. He came once to study the case, then on various other occasions to bring vials and syringes, and a last time, when he said to me: 'Rise and walk.' The pain had disappeared, my breathing was free; I was very weak and hungry, but I got up, and I could walk.

Nevertheless, I did not leave the room for another three weeks. I spent the interminable days lying down, avidly reading the odd assortment of books I managed to lay my hands on: an English grammar in Polish, *Marie Walewska, le tendre amour de Napoléon*, a textbook of elementary trigonometry, *Rouletabille à la rescousse, The Convicts of the Cayenne*, and a curious Nazi propaganda novel, *Die Grosse Heimkehr* ('The Great Repatriation'), which portrayed the tragic destiny of a Galician village of pure German race, oppressed, sacked and finally destroyed by the ferocious Poland of Marshal Beck.

It was sad to be confined within four walls, when outside the air was full of spring and victory, and the wind carried stimulating smells from the nearby woods of moss, fresh grass and mushrooms; and it was humiliating to be dependent on companions for even the most elementary needs, to collect my food from the canteen, and to get water, and in the early days even to change my position in bed.

There were about twenty others in my dormitory, including Leonardo and Cesare; but the most outstanding personality, of more than human stature, was the oldest among them, the Moor from Verona. He must have come from a stock tenaciously attached to the soil, for his real name was Avesani, and he came from Avesa, the launderers' quarter of Verona celebrated by Berto Barbarani.* He was over seventy, and showed all his years; he was a great gnarled old man with

* A dialect poet of Verona of the nineteen-twenties.

huge bones like a dinosaur, tall and upright on his haunches, still as strong as a horse, although age and fatigue had deprived his bony joints of their suppleness. His bald cranium, nobly convex, was encircled at its base with a crown of white hair; but his lean, wrinkled face was of a jaundice-like colour, while his eyes, beneath enormous brows like ferocious dogs lurking at the back of a den, flashed yellow and bloodshot.

In the Moor's chest, skeletal yet powerful, a gigantic but indeterminate anger raged ceaselessly; a senseless anger against everybody and everything, against the Russians and the Germans, against Italy and the Italians, against God and mankind, against himself and us, against day when it was day, and against night when it was night, against his destiny and all destinies, against his trade, even though it was a trade that ran in his blood. He was a bricklayer; for fifty years, in Italy, America, France, then again in Italy, and finally in Germany, he had laid bricks, and every brick had been cemented with curses. He cursed continuously, but not mechanically; he cursed with method and care, acrimoniously, pausing to find the right word, frequently correcting himself, and losing his temper when unable to find the word he wanted; then he cursed the curse that would not come.

It was quite clear that he was possessed by a desperate senile madness; but there was a greatness in his madness, a force and a barbaric dignity, the trampled dignity of beasts in a cage, the dignity that redeemed Capaneus and Caliban.

The Moor hardly ever got up from his bunk. He lay there all day, his enormous, yellow, bony feet sticking out of the end of the bunk half-way across the room; next to him on the floor lay a large shapeless bundle, which none of us ever dared to touch. It contained apparently all his worldly possessions; a heavy woodcutter's axe hung from its outside. Normally, the Moor stared into the distance with bloodshot eyes and stayed silent; but the minimal stimulus was enough, a noise in the corridor, a question asked of him, an incautious brush against his obtrusive feet, an attack of rheumatism; then his deep chest rose up like the sea swelling in a storm, and the mechanism of abuse was once more set in motion.

We respected him, and feared him with a vaguely superstitious fear. Only Cesare approached him, with the impertinent familiarity of a bird scratching about on the craggy back of a rhinoceros, and he amused himself by arousing the Moor's anger with stupid and obscene questions.

Next to the Moor lived the inept Ferrari with his lice, the bottom of the class at the Loreto school. But he was not the only member of the San Vittore confraternity in our dormitory; it was also well represented by Trovati and Cravero.

Trovati, Ambrogio Trovati alias Dusk, was not more than thirty years old; he was of small stature, but muscular and extremely nimble. 'Dusk', he explained to us, was a stage name; he was proud of it, and it fitted him perfectly, for he was a man of a darkened mind, who lived on fanciful expedients in a mental state of perpetual frustrated rebellion. He had passed his adolescence and youth between prison and the stage, and it seemed as if the two institutions were not clearly distinguished in his confused mind. Imprisonment in Germany must finally have tilted the balance.

In his conversation, the true, the possible and the fantastic were intermingled in a varied and inextricable tangle. He spoke of prison and the law courts, as of a theatre, in which nobody is really himself, but everybody is acting, showing off his talents, imitating somebody else, reciting a part; and the theatre, in its turn, was a great obscure symbol, a dark instrument of perdition, the external manifestation of an underground sect, evil and ubiquitous, which rules at everybody's expense, and comes to your home, takes you, puts a mask on you, makes you become what you are not, and do what you do not want to do. This sect is Society; the great enemy, whom he, Dusk, had always fought: he had always been defeated, but had always heroically risen again.

It was Society who had come down to search for him, to challenge him. He used to live in innocence, in a terrestrial paradise; he had been a barber, and had owned his shop, at the time of the visitation. Two messengers had come to tempt him, to propose to him diabolically that he sell his shop and give himself to Art. How well they had known his weak spot; they had flattered him, they had praised the shape of his body, his voice, the expressiveness and mobility of his face. He had resisted twice, three times, then he had given way, and with the address of the film studio in his hand had begun to wander around Milan. But the address was false, they had sent him from door to door; until he had realized that it was a conspiracy. The two messengers had followed him in the background with a movie camera, they had stolen all his words and his gestures of disappointment, and so they had made him an actor without his realizing. They had stolen his image, his shadow, his soul. It was they who had made his sun set, and who had baptized him 'Dusk'.

This was the end for him. He was in their hands: his business sold, no contract, little money, a small part every now and again, a little theft to keep alive. Until his great epopee: fleshy homicide. He had met one of his seducers in a street, and had knifed him; he had become guilty of fleshy homicide, and for this crime had been dragged into court. But he had refused to retain a lawyer, because the whole world was against him, to the last man, and he knew it. Nevertheless, he had been so eloquent, and had presented his case so well, that the Court had acquitted him on the spot with a great ovation, and everyone had wept.

This legendary trial stood at the centre of Trovati's nebulous memory; he relived it at every moment of the day, he spoke of nothing else, and frequently, after dinner in the evening he forced all of us to join him in enacting his trial as a sort of mystery play. He assigned a part to each of us: you the judge, you the prosecutor, you the jury, you the clerk,

103

you the public – everybody was given his part peremptorily. But the accused, and at the same time the defence counsel, was always himself; and when the moment of his torrential harangue arrived, at every performance he explained first, in a rapid 'aside', that fleshy homicide occurs when somebody sticks a knife not into the chest or the stomach, but here, between the heart and the armpit, in the flesh; and it is less serious.*

He would speak without stopping, passionately, for a whole hour, wiping authentic sweat from his brow; then, throwing the folds of a non-existent toga over his left shoulder with a broad gesture, he would conclude: 'On, on, ye snakes, deposit your venom!'

The third former inmate of San Vittore, Cravero from Turin, was, by contrast, an accomplished rogue, uncontaminated, without refinements, one of those rare beings in whom the abstract criminal hypothesis of the penal code seemed to take flesh and human shape. He knew all the jails of Italy well, and had lived in Italy (he admitted it without reserve, in fact with pride) as a thief, burglar and ponce. Possessing such qualities, he had found no difficulty in settling in Germany; he had worked for only one month for the Todt Organization at Berlin, then he had disappeared, ably blending himself into the murky background of the local underworld.

After two or three attempts, he had found the right sort of widow. He helped her with his experience, procured her clients, and took over the financial side of disputed cases, even including knifing; in return she looked after him. He felt himself perfectly at home in that house, despite the difficulties of language, and certain curious habits of his protégée.

When the Russians reached the gates of Berlin, Cravero,

* The descriptive *'omicidio polposo'* ('fleshy homicide') is Trovati's distortion of the technical legal term *'omicidio colposo'* ('homicide without malice aforethought').

who did not like disturbances, weighed anchor, leaving the woman in the lurch, although she burst into tears. He had been overtaken, nevertheless, by the rapid advance and, shifting from camp to camp, had ended up at Katowice. He did not stay there long. In fact, he was the first of the Italians to decide to attempt repatriation by himself. Accustomed as he was to living outside the law, he was not particularly worried by the obstacle of the numerous frontiers he had to pass without documents and of the thousand miles he had to travel without money.

As he was going to Turin, he very courteously offered to take a letter to my home. I accepted, with a certain levity, as will be seen; I accepted because I was ill, because I have great and deep faith in my neighbour, because the Polish post did not work, and because Marya Fyodorovna had paled and changed the subject when I asked her to write a letter on my behalf to be sent to the West.

Cravero left Katowice in the middle of May, and reached Turin in the record time of one month, slipping like an eel through innumerable check-points. He traced my mother, gave her the letter (it was my only sign of life in nine months to reach its destination), and confidentially described to her my extremely worrying state of health; naturally I had not written this in my letter, but I was alone, ill, abandoned, without money, in urgent need of help; in his opinion, I had to be provided for immediately. Certainly it was no easy undertaking; but he, Cravero, my bosom friend, was there to help. If my mother gave him 200,000 lire, he would bring me home to safety in two or three weeks. In fact, if the young lady (my sister, who was listening to the conversation) wanted to accompany him. . . .

It is to my mother's and my sister's credit that they were not wholly taken in by the messenger. They sent him away, asking him to call again in a few days, as they did not have the sum of money available. Cravero went downstairs, stole my sister's bicycle, which was in front of the house, and disappeared. Two years later, at Christmas, he sent me an affectionate greetings card from prison in Turin.

The evenings when Dusk exempted us from rehearsing his trial, Mr Unverdorben took the stage. This strange and attractive name belonged to a mild touchy little old man from Trieste. Mr Unverdorben, who would not reply to anybody who did not call him 'Mr' and who insisted on being addressed with respect, had lived a long adventurous double existence, and like the Moor and Dusk was the prisoner of a dream, in fact of two dreams.

Inexplicably he had survived the Birkenau Lager, and emerged from it with a terrible phlegmon on one foot, and could not walk; so he was the most assiduous and obsequious of those who offered me company and help during my illness. He was also very loquacious, and if he had not repeated himself so frequently, as old men do, his confidences would be enough to make a novel. He was a musician, a great misunderstood musician, a composer and conductor; he had composed a lyric opera, *The Queen of Navarre*, which had been praised by Toscanini; but the manuscript lay unpublished in a drawer, because his enemies had examined his music with such indecent application that in the end they had discovered four consecutive bars in his score which were identical with four in *I Pagliacci*. His good faith was obvious, crystal clear, but the law does not joke about such matters. Three bars yes, four no. Four bars are plagiarism. Mr Unverdorben had been too much of a gentleman to dirty his hands with lawyers and law-suits; in a virile manner, he had said good-bye to art, and had created a new existence for himself as a chef on board transatlantic liners.

He had travelled a lot, and had seen things which no-one else had seen. Above all, he had seen extraordinary animals and plants, and many secrets of nature. He had seen the crocodiles of the Ganges river, which have a single rigid bone running from the tip of the nose to the tail, and which are extremely ferocious and race like the wind; but, because of this singular bone structure, they can only move backwards and forwards like a train on railway lines, and all you have to do to be safe is to place yourself by their side, at a slight angle from their axis.

He had seen the jackals of the Nile, which drink while they run so as not to be bitten by the fish; at night their eyes shine like lanterns, and they sing with raucous human voices. He had also seen Malaysian cabbages which are like our cabbages, but much bigger; if you merely touch their leaves with a finger, you cannot free yourself again; the hand, and then the arm, and then the rash person's entire body is drawn inwards slowly but irresistibly, into the monstrous sticky heart of the carnivorous plant, and digested little by little. The only remedy, which almost nobody knows, is fire, but you have to act quickly; it is enough to light a match under the leaf that has seized its prey, and the plant's grip slowly relaxes. In this way, thanks to his promptness and knowledge of natural history, Mr Unverdorben had saved the captain of his boat from sure death. Then there are certain little black snakes which live buried in the squalid sands of Australia, and which dart out at a man from afar, in the air, like bullets; one bite of theirs is enough to knock out a bull. But everything in nature is balanced, there is no offence without a defence, every poison has its antidote; it is enough to know what it is. The bite of these reptiles is promptly cured if treated with human saliva; but not the saliva of the person who has been attacked. This is why no-one ever travels alone in those parts.

In the long Polish evenings, the air in the dormitory, heavy with tobacco and human smells, was saturated with senseless dreams. This is the most immediate fruit of exile, of uprooting: the prevalence of the unreal over the real. Everyone dreamed past and future dreams, of slavery and redemption, of improbable paradises, of equally mythical and improbable enemies; cosmic enemies, perverse and subtle, who pervade everything like the air. Everyone, except perhaps Cravero, and certainly D'Agata.

D'Agata had no time to dream, because he was obsessed by the fear of bugs. Of course, nobody liked these unpleasant companions; but in the end we had all grown accustomed to them. They were not few and scattered, but a compact army, which invaded all our pallets at springtime; during the day they nestled in the chinks of the walls and in the wooden bunks, and as soon as the confusion of the day died down, they sallied forth. We would willingly have ceded them a small portion of our blood; it was less easy to accustom ourselves to feel them running furtively over our faces and bodies, under our clothes. The only people to sleep peacefully were those who were fortunate enough to be heavy sleepers, and who managed to fall into unconsciousness before the bugs woke up.

D'Agata, who was a minute, sober, reserved and extremely clean Sicilian bricklayer, was forced to sleep by day, and spent the nights perching on his bed, staring around, his eyes dilated with horror, insomnia, and spasmodic concentration. He clutched a rudimentary tool in his hand, which he had constructed from a stick and a piece of wire grating, and the wall next to him was covered with a lurid constellation of bloody spots.

At first, these habits of his had been derided; was his skin thinner than ours? But then compassion had prevailed, mixed with a trace of envy; because, of all of us, D'Agata was the only one whose enemy was concrete, present, tangible, capable of being fought, beaten, crushed against the wall.

8. Southwards

I HAD BEEN walking for hours in the marvellous morning air, drawing it deeply into my battered lungs like medicine. I was not very steady on my feet, but I felt an imperious need to take possession of my body again, to re-establish a contact, by now broken for almost two years, with trees and grass, with the heavy brown soil in which one could feel the seeds chafing, with the ocean of air wafting the pollen from the fir trees, wave upon wave, from the Carpathians to the black streets of the mining city.

I had been wandering around like this for a week now, exploring the environs of Katowice. The pleasant weakness of convalescence ran through my veins. At the same time, powerful doses of insulin also ran through my veins, prescribed, found, bought and injected in agreement by Leonardo and Gottlieb. While I walked, the insulin carried out its prodigious work in silence; it ran through my blood searching for sugar, took care of its diligent combustion and conversion into energy, and distracted it from other less proper destinies. But there was not much sugar available; suddenly, dramatically, almost always at the same time, the supplies ran out; then my legs folded under me, everything grew black and I was forced to sit on the ground wherever I was, frozen and overwhelmed by an attack of ferocious hunger. At this point, the labours and gifts of my third protector, Marya Fyodorovna Prima, came to my aid; I took a packet of glucose from my pocket and swallowed it greedily. After a few minutes, light returned, the sun grew warm once more and I could begin my walk again.

When I returned to the camp that morning, I came on an

unusual scene. In the middle of the square stood Captain Egorov, surrounded by a dense crowd of Italians. He was holding a large revolver, which, however, he only used to emphasize the salient parts of the discourse he was making with broad gestures. Very little of his speech could be understood. Basically only two words, because he repeated them frequently; but these two words were heavenly messengers: 'Ripatriatsiya' and 'Odyessa'.

So, we were to be repatriated via Odessa; we were to return home. The whole camp instantly ran wild. Captain Egorov was lifted from the ground, revolver and all, and carried precariously in triumph. People bellowed in the corridors: 'Home! home!'; others turned to their luggage, making as much noise as possible, and throwing rags, waste paper, broken shoes and all sorts of rubbish out of the window. In a few hours the whole camp emptied, under the Olympian eyes of the Russians; some were going to the city to take leave of their girls, others quite simply to paint the town red, others still to spend their last zloty on provisions for the journey or in other more futile ways.

Cesare and I also went to Katowice, with this last programme in mind, carrying our savings and those of five or six comrades in our pockets. For what could we hope to find at the frontier? We did not know, but we had seen enough of the Russians and their ways so far, as to make it seem unlikely that we should find a money exchange at the frontier. So common sense, as well as our euphoric state, counselled us to spend the not excessively large sum we possessed to the very last zloty; to use it all up, for example, in organizing a large Italian-style dinner, based on spaghetti *al burro* which we had not eaten for so long a time.

We walked into a grocery store, placed all our money on the counter, and explained our intentions to the shopkeeper as best we could. I told her, as usual, that I spoke German but was not German; that we were Italians about to leave,

and that we wanted to buy spaghetti, butter, salt, eggs, strawberries and sugar in the most opportune proportions for a
total of exactly sixty-three zloty, not one more nor one less.

The shopkeeper was a wrinkled old woman, with a shrew-
ish and diffident air. She looked at us closely through her
tortoiseshell glasses, then stated flatly, in excellent German,
that according to her we were not Italians at all. First of all,
we spoke German, albeit somewhat badly; then, and above
all, Italians had black hair and passionate eyes, while we
possessed neither. At the most, she would concede that we
were Croats; in fact, now that she thought about it, she had
met some Croats who resembled us. We were, quite indis-
putably, Croats.

I was quite annoyed, and told her abruptly that we were
Italians, whether she liked it or not; Italian Jews, one from
Rome, and one from Turin, who came from Auschwitz and
were going home, and we wanted to buy and spend, and not
waste time in futile discussion.

Jews from Auschwitz? The old woman's look mellowed,
even her lines seemed to soften. That was another matter. She
took us into the back room, made us sit down, offered us two
glasses of real beer, and at once poured forth her legendary
story with pride, her epopee, near in time but already amply
transformed into a *chanson de geste*, refined and polished by
innumerable repetitions.

She was aware of Auschwitz, and everything relating to
Auschwitz interested her, because she had run the risk of
going there. She was not Polish, but German; formerly, she
had owned a shop in Berlin, with her husband. They had
never liked Hitler, and perhaps they had been too incautious
in allowing these singular opinions of theirs to leak out in
the neighbourhood; in 1935 her husband had been taken away
by the Gestapo, and she had never heard of him again. It had
been a terrible blow, but one has to live, and she had continued her business till 1938, when Hitler, '*der Lump*', had

made his famous speech on the radio in which he declared he wanted to start a war.

Then she had grown angry and had written to him. She had written to him personally, 'To Mr Adolf Hitler, Chancellor of the Reich, Berlin', sending him a long letter in which she advised him strongly not to wage war because too many people would be killed, and pointed out to him that if he did he would lose, because Germany could not win against the whole world; even a child could understand that. She had signed the letter with her name, surname and address; then she had settled down to wait.

Five days later the brown-shirts arrived and, on the pretext of carrying out a search, had sacked and turned her house and shop upside down. What did they find? Nothing. She had never meddled in politics; there was only the draft of the letter. Two weeks later they called her to the Gestapo. She thought they would beat her up and send her to the Lager; instead they treated her with loutish contempt, told her they should hang her, but that they were convinced she was only *eine alte blöde Ziege*', a stupid old goat, and that the rope would be wasted on her. However, they had withdrawn her trading licence and had expelled her from Berlin.

She had lived from hand to mouth in Silesia on the black market and other expedients, until, as she had foreseen, the Germans had lost the war. Then, since the whole neighbourhood knew what she had done, the Polish authorities had created no difficulties about granting her a licence for a grocery store. So now she lived in peace, fortified by the thought of how much better the world would be if the rulers of this earth had followed her advice.

At the moment of the departure, Leonardo and I gave back the keys of the surgery and said good-bye to Marya Fyodorovna and Dr Danchenko. Marya appeared silent and sad; I asked her why she did not come to Italy with us, at which she blushed as if I had made a dishonourable proposal. Danchenko intervened; he was carrying a bottle of alcohol and two sheets of paper. At first we thought the alcohol was his personal contribution to the stock of medicaments for the journey, but no, it was for a farewell toast, which was dutifully drunk.

And the sheets of paper? We were amazed to learn that the Command expected from us two declarations of thanks for the humanity and correctness with which we had been treated at Katowice; Danchenko also begged us to mention his name and work explicitly, and to sign the papers, adding the title 'Doctor of Medicine' to our names. This Leonardo was able to do and did; but in my case it was false. I was perplexed, and sought to make Danchenko understand this; but he had no time for formalism such as mine, and rapping his finger on the paper told me angrily not to create difficulties. I signed as he wanted; who was I to deprive him of a little help in his career?

But the ceremony was not yet over. Danchenko in turn took out two testimonials written in a beautiful hand on two sheets of lined paper, evidently torn from an exercise book. My testimonial declared with unconstrained generosity that 'Primo Levi, doctor of medicine, of Turin, has given able and assiduous help to the Surgery of this Command for four months, and in this manner has merited the gratitude of all the workers of the world.'

The following day our perpetual dream became reality. A train was waiting for us at Katowice station; a long train of goods trucks, which we Italians (about eight hundred) took possession of with cries of delight. First, Odessa; then a fantastic journey by sea through the gates of the Orient; and then Italy.

The prospect of travelling some hundreds of miles in those dilapidated trucks, sleeping on the bare floor, did not worry

113

us at all; nor were we worried by the derisory food supplies provided by the Russians: a little bread, and a packet of soya-bean margarine for each truck. It was a margarine of American origin, heavily salted and as hard as Parmesan cheese; evidently destined for tropical climates, it had finally come into our hands by a series of unimaginable accidents. The rest of our supplies, the Russians assured us with their habitual nonchalance, would be distributed during the journey.

The train, with its cargo of hope, left in the middle of June 1945. There was no escort, no Russian on board; Dr Gottlieb was responsible for the convoy, for he had attached himself spontaneously to us, and had taken on himself the cumulative duties of interpreter, doctor and consul for the itinerant community. We felt in good hands, remote from all doubt or uncertainty; at Odessa the ship was waiting for us.

The journey lasted six days, and if in the course of it we were not forced by hunger to turn beggars or bandits, and in fact reached the end in a reasonably healthy condition, the credit was exclusively Dr Gottlieb's. It became clear immediately after our departure that the Russians of Katowice had sent us on our journey blindly, without making any arrangements with their colleagues at Odessa or at the intermediate stages. When our train stopped at a station (it stopped frequently and for long periods, because regular trains and military transports had precedence), no one knew what to do with us. The stationmasters and the military commanders watched us arrive with doleful surprise, only anxious to rid themselves in turn of our inconvenient presence.

But Gottlieb was there, as sharp as a knife; there was no bureaucratic complication, no barrier of negligence, no official obstinacy which he was unable to remove in a few minutes, each time in a different way. Every difficulty dissolved into mist in the face of his effrontery, his soaring fantasy, his rapier-like quickness. He came back from each encounter with the monster of a thousand faces, which lives wherever official forms and circulars gather, radiant with victory like St George after his duel with the dragon, and recounted the rapid exchange, too conscious of his superiority to glory in it.

The local stationmaster, for example, had demanded our travel warrant, which notoriously did not exist; Gottlieb told him that he was going to pick it up, and entered the telegraph office nearby, where he fabricated one in a few moments, written in the most convincing of official jargon, on some scrap of paper which he so plastered with stamps, seals and illegible signatures as to make it as holy and venerable as an authentic emanation from the Top. Another time he had gone to the Quartermaster's office of a Kommandantur and had respectfully informed him that eight hundred Italians had arrived in the station with nothing to eat. The Quartermaster replied '*nichevò*', his stores were empty, he needed an authorization, he would see to it tomorrow; and he clumsily tried to throw him out, like some importunate mendicant; but Gottlieb smiled, and said to him: 'Comrade, you haven't understood me. These Italians *must* be fed, and today, because this is what Stalin wants'; provisions arrived in a flash.

But for me the journey became a boundless torment. I must have recovered from my pleurisy, but my body was in open rebellion, and seemed to scoff at the doctors and their medicines. Every night, during my sleep, fever swept treacherously through me; an intense fever of unknown nature, which reached its peak near dawn. I used to wake up prostrate, only semi-conscious, and with a wrist, an elbow, or a knee numbed by stabbing pains. Then I was only capable of lying on the floor of the truck or on the platform, a prey to delirium and pain until about midday; after which, within a few hours, everything returned to normal, and towards evening I felt almost well. Leonardo and Gottlieb looked at me perplexed and helpless.

The train ran through endless fields, sombre towns and villages, dense wild forests which I thought had disappeared thousands of years before from the heart of Europe; the conifers and birches were so thick that they were forced desperately upwards, competing for the light of the sun in an oppressive verticality. The train forced its way as if in a tunnel, in green-black gloom, amid bare smooth trunks, under the high continuous roof of thickly intertwined branches. Rzeszów, Przemyśl with its grim fortifications, Lemberg (Lvov).

At Lemberg, a skeleton city, destroyed by bombardment and the war, the train stopped for an entire night in a deluge of rain. The roof of our truck was not watertight; we had to get down and look for shelter. We and a few others could find nothing better than the service subway: dark, two inches of mud, with ferocious draughts. But as punctual as ever, my fever arrived in the middle of the night, like a merciful blow on the head, bringing me the ambiguous benefit of unconsciousness.

Ternopol, Proskurov. The train reached Proskurov at dusk, the engine was uncoupled, and Gottlieb assured us that we should not leave until the morning. So we prepared to sleep overnight in the station. The waiting-room was very large; Cesare, Leonardo, Daniele and I took possession of one corner, Cesare left for the village in his capacity as purveyor, and returned soon afterwards with eggs, lettuce and a packet of tea.

We lit a fire on the floor (we were not the only ones, nor the first; the room was covered with the remains of the innumerable bivouacs of people who had preceded us, and the ceiling and walls were black with smoke, as in an old kitchen). Cesare cooked the eggs, and prepared plenty of well-sugared tea.

Now, either that tea was far more robust than the sort we were used to, or Cesare had mistaken the quantity; because in a short time we lost every trace of sleep and tiredness, and felt ourselves kindled into an unusual mood – tense and alert, hilarious, lucid and sensitive. As a result, every act and every word of that night has remained impressed on my memory, and I can recall it as if it were yesterday.

Daylight disappeared with extreme slowness, at first pink, then violet, then grey, followed by the silvery splendour of a warm moonlit night. While we were smoking and talking gaily, two young girls, dressed in black, were sitting next to us on a wooden box. They were speaking together; not in Russian, but in Yiddish.

'Do you understand what they're saying?' asked Cesare.

'A few words.'

'Up and at 'em, then. See if they'll play.'

That night everything seemed easy to me, even understanding Yiddish. With unaccustomed boldness, I turned to the girls, greeted them and, trying to imitate their pronunciation, asked them in German if they were Jewish, and declared that we four were also Jewish. The girls (they were perhaps sixteen or eighteen years old) burst out laughing. '*Ihr sprecht keyn Jiddisch; ihr seyd ja keyne Jiden!*' 'you do not speak Yiddish; so you cannot be Jews!' In their language, the phrase amounted to rigorous logic.

Yet we really were Jews, I explained. Italian Jews: Jews in Italy, and in all Western Europe, do not speak Yiddish.

This was a great novelty for them, a comic oddity, as if someone had affirmed that there are Frenchmen who do not speak French. I tried to recite to them the beginning of the *Shema*, the basic Hebrew prayer; their incredulity grew weaker, but their merriment increased. Who had ever heard Hebrew pronounced in so ridiculous a way?

The elder one's name was Sore; she had a small, sharp, mischievous face, rotund and full of asymmetrical dimples; our difficult, halting conversation seemed to cause her piquant amusement, and stimulated her like tickling.

But if we were Jews, then so were all those others, she said to me, pointing with a circular gesture to the eight hundred Italians who filled the room. What difference was there between us and them? The same language, the same faces, the same clothing. No, I explained to her; they were Christians, they came from Genoa, Naples, Sicily; perhaps some of them had Arab blood in their veins. Sore looked around perplexed; this was extremely confusing. In her country things were much clearer: a Jew was a Jew, and a Russian was a Russian, there were no two ways about it.

They were two refugees, she explained to me. They came from Minsk, in White Russia; when the Germans had drawn near, their family had asked to be transferred to the interior of the Soviet Union, to escape the slaughter of the Einsatz-kommandos of Eichmann. Their request had been carried out to the letter; they had all been sent three thousand miles from their town, to Samarcand in Uzbekistan, near the Roof of the World, in sight of mountains twenty thousand feet high. She and her sister were still children at the time; then their mother had died, and their father had been mobilized for service on a frontier. The two of them had learnt Uzbek, and many other fundamental things: how to live from day to day, how to travel across continents with a small suitcase between the two of them, in fact how to live like the fowls of the air, who labour not, neither do they spin, and who take no thought for the morrow.

Such were Sore and her silent sister. Like us, they were returning home. They had left Samarcand in March, and had set out on the journey like feathers abandoning themselves to the wind. They had travelled, partly in trucks and partly on foot, across the Kara-kum, the Desert of the Black Sand; they had arrived at Krasnovodsk on the Caspian Sea by train, and there they had waited until a fishing boat took them to Baku. From Baku they had continued by any means they happened to find, for they had no money, only an unlimited faith in the future and in their neighbour, and a natural virgin love of life.

Everybody around was sleeping; Cesare listened to the conversation restlessly, occasionally asking me if the preliminaries were over and if we were getting down to brass tacks; then, disappointed, he went outside in search of more concrete adventures.

At about midnight the quiet of the waiting-room, and the girls' story, were abruptly interrupted. A door, connecting the large room by a small corridor to another smaller one, reserved for soldiers in transit, flew open violently, as if blown by a gust of wind. On the threshold appeared a Russian soldier, almost a boy, drunk; he looked around with absent eyes, then started forward, head lowered, lurching fearfully, as if the floor had suddenly tilted under him. Three Soviet officers were standing in the corridor, engaged in conversation. The boy soldier braked as he reached them, drew himself stiffly to attention, and gave a military salute, which the three returned with dignity. Then off he started again, moving in semicircles like a skater, cleared the outside door miraculously, and could be heard vomiting and gulping noisily on the platform. He came back with a slightly less uncertain step, once more saluted the impassive officers and disappeared. After a quarter of an hour, the identical scene was repeated, as if in a nightmare: dramatic entrance, pause, salute, hasty crooked journey across the sleepers' legs towards the open air, evacuation, return, salute; and so on for an infinite number of times, at regular intervals, without the three ever giving him more than a distrait glance and a correct salute.

So that memorable night passed until my fever conquered me once more; then I lay on the ground, shivering silently. Gottlieb came, and brought with him an unusual medicine: half a litre of raw vodka, illicitly distilled, which he had bought from some peasants; it tasted of must, vinegar and fire. 'Drink it,' he told me, 'drink it all. It will do you good, and in any case we have nothing else here for your illness.'

I drank the infernal philtre not without an effort, burning my mouth and throat, and in a short time fell into a state of nothingness. When I woke up the following morning, I felt oppressed by a heavy weight; but it was not the fever, nor a bad dream. I lay buried under a layer of other sleepers, in a sort of human incubator of people who had arrived during the night and who could find room only on top of those already lying on the floor.

I was thirsty; thanks to the combined action of the vodka and animal warmth, I must have lost pints of sweat. The singular cure was wholly successful; the fever and pains had definitely disappeared, and returned no more.

The train left, and in a few hours we reached Zhmerinka, a railway junction two hundred miles from Odessa. Here a great surprise and fierce disappointment awaited us. Gottlieb, who had conferred there with the military Command, went along the train, truck by truck, and informed us that we should all have to get off: the train was going no farther.

Why was it going no farther? And how and when would we reach Odessa? 'I don't know,' replied Gottlieb, embarrassed: 'nobody knows. I only know that we have to get off the train, settle ourselves somehow on the platform, and await orders.' He was very pale and visibly disturbed.

We got down, and spent the night in the station; Gottlieb's defeat, the first one, seemed to us a bad omen. The next morning our guide, together with his inseparable brother and brother-in-law, had disappeared. They had vanished into emptiness, with all their conspicuous luggage; somebody said he had seen them talking to Russian railwaymen, and in the night climbing on to a military train going back from Odessa to the Polish border.

We stayed at Zhmerinka for three days, oppressed by a

sense of uneasiness, frustration or terror, according to our temperaments and the scraps of information we managed to extort from the Russians there. They manifested no surprise at our fate and our enforced stop, and replied to our questions in the most disconcerting of ways. One Russian told us that it was true, that various ships had left Odessa with English or American soldiers who were being repatriated, and that we also would embark sooner or later; we had food to eat, Hitler was no more, so why were we complaining? Another one told us that the previous week a trainload of Frenchmen, travelling to Odessa, had been stopped at Zhmerinka and directed towards the north 'because the railway lines were cut'. A third one informed us that he had personally seen a trainload of German prisoners travelling towards the Far East; the matter was clear, according to him, for were we not also allies of the Germans? All right then, they were sending us as well to dig trenches on the Japanese front.

To complicate matters another trainload of Italians coming from Rumania arrived at Zhmerinka on the third day. They looked totally different from us; there were about six hundred men and women, well dressed, with suitcases and trunks, some with cameras slung round their necks – almost tourists. They looked down on us, like poor relations; so far they had travelled in a regular train of passenger coaches, paying for their tickets, and were in order as regards their passports, money, travel documents and collective permit for Italy via Odessa. If only we could gain permission from the Russians to join up with them, then we too should reach Odessa.

With much condescension, they gave us to understand that they were persons of consequence; they were civilian and military officials from the Italian Legation at Bucharest, as well as certain other persons who, after the ARMIR* had been dissolved, had stayed in Rumania with various duties, or to fish in troubled waters. There were whole family groups

* Italian Army in Russia.

among them, husbands with lawfully-wedded Rumanian wives and numerous children.

But the Russians, in contrast to the Germans, possess little talent for subtle distinctions and classifications. A few days later we were all travelling together towards the north, towards an unknown goal, at all events towards a new exile. Italian-Rumanians and Italian-Italians, all in the same cattle trucks, all sick at heart, all in the hands of the inscrutable Soviet bureaucracy, an obscure and gigantic power, not ill-intentioned towards us, but suspicious, negligent, stupid, contradictory and in effect as blind as the forces of nature.

9. Northwards

IN THE FEW days we spent at Zhmerinka we were reduced to penury; this, in those conditions, was in itself not particularly tragic, compared with the far more serious prospect of an imminent departure for an unknown destination. Lacking the shelter provided by Gottlieb's talent for improvisation, we had undergone the full impact of the 'Rumanians'' superior economic power; they could pay five, ten times as much as we could for any goods, and did so, because they too had exhausted their food supplies, and they too foresaw that we should be leaving for a place where money would count for little, and where it would be difficult to keep it.

We had encamped at the station, and often made expeditions to the village, which consisted of low, unequal houses, built with a curious and amusing contempt for geometry and uniformity: nearly aligned façades, near vertical walls, near right angles; but here and there a pillar was to be found, resembling a column, with a pretentious capital and volutes. Thick thatched roofs covered smoky, gloomy interiors, where one coùld glimpse the enormous central stove with straw mattresses for sleeping, and the black icons in a corner. At a crossroad a gigantic, white-haired, barefoot storyteller recited; he stared at the sky with his blind eyes, and at intervals bent his head and made the sign of the cross on his forehead with his thumb.

In the main street, fixed on two stakes driven into the muddy soil, stood a wooden plaque with a map of Europe painted on it, now fading from the sun and rains of many a summer. It must have been used to follow the war bulletins, but it had been painted from memory, as if seen from a great distance; France was decidedly a coffee pot, the Iberian Peninsula a head in profile, with the nose sticking out from Portugal, and Italy a genuine boot, just a trifle oblique, with the sole and heel smooth and straightlined. Only four cities were shown in Italy: Rome, Venice, Naples and Dronero.

Zhmerinka was a large agricultural village, formerly a market town, as could be deduced from the huge central square, of trodden earth, with numerous parallel rows of iron bars to which beasts could be tethered. It was now wholly empty; but in a corner, in the shade of an oak tree, a tribe of nomads had encamped, a vision stemming from distant millennia.

Both men and women were dressed in goatskins, tied to their limbs with leather thongs; on their feet they wore slippers made from the bark of birch trees. There were several families, about twenty people, and their home was an enormous cart, as massive as some instrument of war, constructed of beams crudely squared and mortised, resting on heavy wheels of solid wood; the four shaggy carthorses to be seen grazing nearby must have had a hard time dragging it. Who were they, where did they come from, and where were they going? We did not know; but in those days we felt that they were singularly close to us, blown like us by the wind, dependent like us on the fickleness of a distant, unknown, erratic will, symbolized in the wheels dragging us and them, in the stupid perfection of the circle which has neither beginning nor end.

Not far from the square, near the railway, we came across another apparition heavy with foreboding. We saw a depot of logs, massive and rough like everything in that country where the subtle and refined have no place; among the logs, beaten to the ground by the sun, cooked by the sun, lay a dozen German prisoners, like unattended cattle. No-one guarded them, no-one commanded them, or looked after them; as far as we could see, they had been forgotten, simply abandoned to their fate.

They were dressed in rags, which were faded but still recognizable as the proud uniforms of the Wehrmacht. They had pinched, dazed, wild faces; accustomed to live, act, and fight within the iron bounds of Authority, their support and sustenance, they found themselves impotent and inanimate when Authority itself ceased. These good subjects, good executors of all commands, good instruments of power, did not possess even a particle of power in themselves; they were emptied and inert, like barren leaves piled up by the wind in sheltered corners; they had not even sought safety in flight.

They saw us, and some of them moved towards us with the uncertain steps of automata. They asked for bread; not in their own language, but in Russian. We refused, because our bread was precious. But Daniele did not refuse; Daniele, whose strong wife, whose brother, parents and no less than thirty relatives had been killed by the Germans; Daniele, who was the sole survivor of the raid on the Venice ghetto, and who from the day of the liberation had fed on grief, took out a piece of bread, showed it to these phantoms, and placed it on the ground. But he insisted that they come to get it dragging themselves on all fours; which they did, docilely.

It must have been true that groups of Allied ex-prisoners had embarked at Odessa months before, as some Russians had told us, for the station of Zhmerinka, our temporary and scarcely intimate residence, still bore the signs: a triumphal arch made of branches, now withered, bearing the words 'Long live the United Nations'; enormous ghastly portraits of Stalin, Roosevelt and Churchill, with phrases extolling the victory against the common enemy. But the brief season of concord between the three great allies must now have been drawing to its end, for the paintings were discoloured and faded by the weather, and were taken down during our stay. A painter arrived; he put up scaffolding along the wall of the station, and covered the slogan 'Workers of the world, unite!' with a coating of whitewash; in its place we saw, with a subtle sense of chill, another quite different slogan appear, letter by letter: '*Vpered na Zapàd*', 'On towards the West'.

The repatriation of Allied soldiers had now finished, but other trains arrived and left for the south before our eyes. These were also Russian trains but quite distinct from the military ones, glorious and homely, which we had seen passing through Katowice. They were trainloads of Ukrainian women returning from Germany; only women, because the men had gone off as soldiers or partisans, or else had been killed by the Germans.

Their exile had been different from ours, and from that of the prisoners of war. Not all of them, but the majority, had abandoned their homes 'spontaneously'. A coerced, black-mailed spontaneity, distorted by subtle and heavy Nazi lies and propaganda, both threatening and enticing, blaring out from the radio, newspapers, posters; nevertheless, a demonstration of free will, an assent. Women aged sixteen to forty, hundreds of thousands of them, peasant women, students, factory workers, had left the devastated fields, the closed schools and bombarded factories for the invaders' bread. Not a few were mothers, who had left to earn bread for their children. In Germany they had found bread, barbed wire, hard work, German order, servitude and shame; now under the weight of their shame they were being repatriated, without joy and without hope.

Victorious Russia had no forgiveness for them. They returned home in roofless cattle trucks, which were divided horizontally by boards so as to exploit the space better: sixty, eighty women to a truck. They had no luggage, only the worn-out discoloured clothes they were wearing. If their young bodies were still solid and healthy, their closed and bitter faces, their evasive eyes displayed a disturbing, animal-like humiliation and resignation; not a voice emerged from those coils of limbs, which sluggishly untangled themselves when the train stopped at the station. No-one was waiting for them, no-one seemed aware of them. Their inertia, their fugitive shyness, their painful lack of pudency, was that of humiliated and tame beasts. We alone watched their passage, with compassion and sadness, a new testimony to, and a new aspect of, the pestilence which had prostrated Europe.

We left Zhmerinka at the end of June, oppressed by a deep anguish born of disillusionment and uncertainty about our destiny which had found an obscure echo and confirmation in the scenes we had witnessed.

We were fourteen hundred Italians, including the 'Rumanians'. We were loaded on to about thirty goods trucks, which were tacked on to a northbound train. At Zhmerinka nobody knew or was prepared to tell us our destination; but we were going northwards, away from the sea, away from Italy, towards exile, solitude, gloom, winter. Despite this, we thought it a good sign that provisions were not distributed for the journey; perhaps it would not be a long one.

In fact we only travelled for two days and one night, with very few stops, through a majestic and monotonous scenery of desert steppes, forests, forlorn villages and wide slow rivers. It was uncomfortable, crushed in the goods trucks; on the first evening, taking advantage of a halt, Cesare and I got out to stretch our legs and find some more satisfactory arrangement. At the head of the train we saw several passenger carriages, and a hospital car; it seemed empty. 'Why don't we climb in?' proposed Cesare. 'It's not allowed,' I replied foolishly. Why in fact should it be forbidden, and by whom? In any case, on various occasions we had noticed already that the Western religion (German in particular) of differential prohibitions has no deep roots in Russia.

The hospital car was not only empty, but offered sybaritic refinements. Washbasins which worked, with water and soap; first-rate suspension to absorb the jarring of the wheels; wonderful bunks resting on adjustable springs, complete with white sheets and warm blankets. At the head of the bed I chose, I even found, as an additional gift of the gods, a book in Italian: *I Ragazzi di Via Paal*, which I had never read as a child. While our companions were already declaring us lost, we enjoyed a heavenly night.

The train crossed the River Beresina at the end of the second day, as the sun, garnet red, sank obliquely between the tree trunks with bewitching slowness, casting a blood-red glow on the waters, the woods and the battle-strewn plain. The journey ended a few hours later, in the middle of the night, at the height of a violent storm. We had to climb down in a deluge, in total darkness, lit momentarily by flashes of lightning. We walked for half an hour in single file through the grass and mud, each of us like a blind man, holding on to the man in front, while heaven knows whom the leader of the column followed; finally, soaked to the skin, we emerged at a huge dark edifice, half destroyed by bombardment. The rain continued, the floor was muddy and wet, and more water came through the holes in the roof; we waited for day in a state of exhaustion and passive drowsiness.

The dawn arose in splendour. We went outside, and only then could we see that we had spent the night in the pit of a theatre, in the middle of a large Soviet military camp which had been destroyed and abandoned. All the buildings had been subjected to a Teutonically methodical devastation and plundering; the German armies in flight had carried away everything that could be carried: locks, bars, railings, the entire lighting and heating plant, the water pipes, even the fence-posts. Not a nail had been left in the walls. The tracks and sleepers of a nearby railway junction had been torn up: with a special machine, the Russians told us.

In short, it was more than a sack: it was the genius of destruction, of anti-creation, here as at Auschwitz; it was the mystique of barrenness, beyond all demands of war or impulse for booty.

But they had not been able to carry away the unforgettable frescoes which covered the inside walls: the work, naïve, forceful and crude, of some anonymous soldier-poet. Three gigantic horsemen, armed with swords, helmets and clubs, stood on a hill, turning their eyes towards an endless horizon of virgin lands to be conquered. Stalin, Lenin, Molotov, reproduced with reverent affection in intent, with sacrilegious audacity in effect, and really only recognizable by their respective moustache, pointed beard and spectacles. Then there was an enormous spider, at the centre of a web as large as the wall, with a lock of black hair across one eye, a swastika on its rump, and written underneath: 'Death to Hitler's invaders'. A Soviet soldier in chains, tall and blond, raised a handcuffed arm to judge his judges; these, hundreds of them all against one, huddled on the benches of the amphitheatre-court, like so many repellent men-insects, with yellow and grey faces, twisted, distorted, as macabre as skulls, cringing against each other, like lemurs fleeing the light, driven back into nothingness by the prophetic gesture of the prisoner-hero.

In these spectral barracks, and spilling outside over the vast courtyards overgrown with grass, thousands of foreigners bivouacked, in transit like us, belonging to all the nations of Europe.

The generous warmth of the sun began to penetrate the damp soil, and mist arose from everything. I walked a few hundred yards away from the theatre, entering an overgrown meadow where I intended to strip and dry myself in the sun; and in the middle of the meadow, as if he were waiting for me, whom should I see but Mordo Nahum, my Greek, almost unrecognizable in his opulent fatness and the quasi-Soviet uniform he was wearing; he looked at me with his pale owlish eyes, lost in his round rosy, red-bearded face.

He greeted me with fraternal cordiality, disregarding a spiteful question of mine about the United Nations who had taken so little care of him and his Greeks. He asked me how I was; did I need anything? Food? Clothes? Yes, I could not deny it, I had need of many things. 'It will be seen to,' he replied mysteriously and magnanimously; 'here I count for something.' He paused briefly, and added, 'Do you need a woman?'

I looked at him dumbfounded; I was afraid I had not understood him. But the Greek, with a broad gesture, swept three-quarters of the horizon with his hand: and then I saw that in the middle of the tall grass, idly stretched out in the sun, far and near, lay some twenty huge sleepy girls. They were blonde and rosy creatures, with powerful backs, massive frames and placid bovine faces, dressed in various primitive and incongruous styles. 'They come from Bessarabia,' the Greek explained to me: 'they are all employees of mine. The Russians like them like this, white and substantial. There was a great *pagaille*, a great muddle here before I arrived but since I have taken over, everything has been running smoothly: cleanliness, choice, discretion and no quarrels about money. It's also a good business: and sometimes, *moi aussi j'y prends mon plaisir.*'

I now recalled, in a new light, the episode of the hard-boiled egg, and the indignant challenge of the Greek: 'Come on, tell me an article I have never dealt in!' No, I had no need of a woman, or at least not in that sense. After a cordial conversation, we went our ways; and since then, with the subsiding of the whirlwind which had upturned this old Europe, dragging it into a savage quadrille of separations and encounters, I have never again seen my Greek master, nor have I ever heard further of him.

10. The Little Hen

THE ASSEMBLY CAMP where I had so unexpectedly found
Mordo Nahum was called Slutsk. Anyone searching for the
village bearing this name on a good map of the Soviet Union
could find it with a little care, in White Russia, about sixty
miles south of Minsk. But the village called Starye Dorogi,
our final destination, is not to be found on any map.

In July 1945, about ten thousand persons were resident at
Slutsk; I say persons, because any more restrictive term
would be inappropriate. There were men, but also a good
number of women and children. There were Catholics,
Jews, Orthodox Christians and Muslims; there were people
with white and with yellow skins and Negroes in American
uniform; Germans, Poles, French, Greeks, Dutch, Italians
and others; and in addition, Germans pretending to be
Austrians, Austrians declaring themselves Swiss, Russians
stating that they were Italians, a woman dressed as a man, and
finally, conspicuous in the midst of this ragged crowd, a
Magyar general in full uniform, as quarrelsome, motley and
stupid as a cock.

Slutsk was comfortable. It was hot, excessively so; we slept
on the ground, but there was no work to be done and there
was food for everybody. In fact, the canteen was wonderful;
the Russians entrusted it, for one week in rotation, to each
of the principal nationalities represented in the camp. We ate
in a huge room, clean and full of light; each table was laid
for eight; all one had to do was to arrive at the correct time
and sit down, without controls or shifts or queues, and the
procession of voluntary cooks arrived at once, with surprising
foods, bread and tea. During our brief stay the Hungarians

were in office: they made fiery goulashes, and enormous portions of spaghetti with parsley, overcooked and crazily sugared. Moreover, faithful to their national idols, they had instituted a gypsy orchestra; six peasant musicians, in corduroy trousers and embroidered leather doublets, majestic and sweating, began with the Soviet national anthem, then the Hungarian and the *Hatikva* (in honour of the large nucleus of Hungarian Jews), and continued with interminable frivolous Tziganes until the last diner had laid down his fork.

The camp was not fenced. It consisted of broken-down buildings, of one or two storeys, aligned along the four sides of a vast grassy square, probably the old parade ground. Under the burning sun of the hot Russian summer, the square was filled with clusters of people sleeping or intent on delousing themselves, mending their clothes, or cooking on improvised fires; the scene was animated by more energetic groups, playing football or ninepins. An enormous wooden hut, low and square, with three entrances all on the same side, dominated the centre. On the three architraves, an uncertain hand had painted in large Cyrillic characters, three words: *Mushskaya, Shenskaya, Ofitserskaya,* 'For men', 'For women', 'For officers'. It was the camp latrine, and at the same time its most salient feature. On the inside, there was only a floor with loose planks, and a hundred square holes, ten by ten, like a gigantic Rabelaisian multiplication table. There were no sub-divisions between the sections allotted to the three sexes; or if there once had been, they had disappeared.

The Russian administration took no care at all of the camp, so that one wondered if it really existed; but it must have existed, since we ate every day. In other words, it was a good administration.

We spent ten days at Slutsk. They were empty days, without encounters, without events to anchor the memory. One day we tried to leave the rectangle of barracks, and enter the plain to collect herbs to eat; but after half an hour's walk we found ourselves as if in the middle of the sea, at the centre of the horizon, without a tree, a hill, a house to choose as goal. The immense, heroic space of Russia gave a sense of giddiness to us Italians, accustomed as we were to a landscape of mountains and hills and a plain alive with the presence of man, and weighed down our hearts with painful memories. Later we tried to cook the herbs we had collected, but we got very little from them.

In an attic, I had found a textbook on obstetrics, in German, with good coloured illustrations, in two heavy volumes; and as printed paper is a vice of mine, and I had abstained for more than a year, I passed my time reading desultorily, or else sleeping in the sun amid the wild grass.

One morning, the news spread among us, with mysterious and lightning speed, that we should have to leave Slutsk, on foot, to settle at Starye Dorogi, forty-five miles away, in a camp for Italians only. The Germans, in analogous circumstances, would have covered the walls with bilingual placards, beautifully printed, specifying the hour of departure, the prescribed equipment, the time-table, and threatening deserters with the death penalty. The Russians, in contrast, allowed the ordinance to spread by itself, and the march to the other camp to organize itself.

The news provoked something of an uproar. In ten more or less comfortable days, we had settled down at Slutsk, and above all we feared leaving the extravagant abundance of the Slutsk kitchens for some unknown miserable condition. Moreover, forty-five miles are a lot; none of us was trained for so long a march, and few possessed suitable shoes. We tried in vain to obtain more precise information from the Russian Command; all we managed to find out was that we should have to leave on the morning of 20th July, and that a real Russian Command apparently did not exist.

On the morning of 20th July we collected in the main square, like an immense band of gypsies. At the last moment, it had emerged that Slutsk and Starye Dorogi were linked by rail; however, only the women and children, as well as the usual protégés, and the no less usual fast operators were allowed to travel by train. In fact, it did not need exceptional cunning to get round the tenuous bureaucracy ruling our fate; but not many of us were aware of this at the time.

The order to leave was given at about ten o'clock, followed immediately by a counter-order. After this, numerous other false departures followed, so that we began to move only about midday, without eating.

A large motorway runs from Slutsk to Starye Dorogi, the same one connecting Warsaw to Moscow. At that time it was wholly abandoned; it consisted of two lateral carriageways, of bare earth, meant for horses, and a central carriageway, formerly asphalted but ruined by explosions and the tracks of armoured vehicles, and consequently little different from the other two. It ran across an endless plain, almost without villages, and as a result it consisted of enormously long straight stretches; between Slutsk and Starye Dorogi there was only one curve, barely perceptible.

We had set out in a rather carefree mood; the weather was magnificent, we were quite well fed, and the idea of a long walk in the heart of this legendary area, the Pripet marshes, had a certain fascination in itself. But we soon changed our minds.

In no other part of Europe, I think, can you walk for ten hours, and always remain at the same place, as if in a nightmare: always with the same straight road in front of you, stretching to the horizon, always the same steppe and forests on both sides, and behind your back yet more road stretching to the other horizon, like a ship's wake; not a village, or a house, or smoke, or a milestone to show in some way that a bit of space had been conquered; not a living creature to meet, except for flights of crows and an occasional hawk cruising idly in the wind.

After a few hours' march, our column, initially compact, stretched for one or two miles. A Russian military cart brought up the rear drawn by two horses and driven by a hideous scowling N.C.O.; he had lost both lips in battle, and his face was a terrifying skull from nose to chin. I think his duty was to pick up anyone exhausted; instead, he was diligently engaged in picking up the luggage gradually dropped by the wayside by people too weary to carry it any farther. For a while we deluded ourselves that he would give it back on arrival; but the first person who tried to stop and wait for the cart was greeted with shouts, cracks of the whip and inarticulate threats. This was how my two volumes of obstetrics ended, for they constituted far and away the heaviest part of my personal luggage.

By dusk, our group was now walking alone. Besides myself, there was the mild and patient Leonardo; Daniele, limping and furious from thirst and tiredness; Mr Unverdorben, with a Triestine friend of his; and, naturally, Cesare.

We stopped for a rest at the only curve breaking the relentless monotony of the road; there was a roofless hut, perhaps the only visible remains of a village swept away by the war. Behind it, we discovered a well, where we quenched our thirst greedily. We were tired, with swollen blistered feet. I had lost my archiepiscopal shoes long before, and had inherited, heaven knows from whom, a pair of cyclist's plimsolls, as light as a feather; but they were tight, and I was forced to take them off at intervals and walk barefoot.

We held a brief council: what if he made us walk all night? It would be hardly surprising; at Katowice once, the Russians had made us unload boots from a train for twenty-four hours on end, and they had also worked with us. Why not desert and hide in the forest? We would reach Starye Dorogi the next day at our leisure, the N.C.O. certainly had no roll call, the night was warm, there was water, and between the six of us we had something for dinner, although not very much. The hut was in ruins, but there was still a bit of roof to shelter us from the dew.

'Excellent,' said Cesare, 'I'm all for it. I'm going to have roast chicken this evening.' So we hid in the wood until the cart with the skeleton had passed by, waited for the last laggers to leave the well, and took possession of our bivouac for the night. We spread our blankets on the ground, opened our sacks, lit a fire, and began to prepare dinner, with bread, *kasha* of millet and a tin of peas.

'To hell with your dinner!' said Cesare; 'to hell with your peas! Now get this: I want to hold a party this evening, and I'm going to have roast chicken.'

Cesare is an untameable man; I had already realized this from wandering around the markets of Katowice with him. It was useless to point out to him what a senseless idea it was searching for a chicken at night, in the middle of the Pripet marshes, without knowing Russian and without money to pay for it. It was useless to offer him a double ration of *kasha* to shut him up. 'You stay here with your bloody *kasha*; I'm going to look for my chicken by myself, and that's the last you'll see of me. So goodbye to you and the Russians and the hut; I'm off, and returning to Italy by myself. Perhaps via Japan.'

At that point I offered to accompany him. Not because of the chicken or the threats; but because I am fond of Cesare, and I enjoy watching him at work.

'Bravo, Lapè,' cried Cesare. Lapè is me; so Cesare baptized me long ago and so he still calls me, for the following reason. Our hair was, of course, shaved off in the Lager; at the liberation, after a year of cropping, everybody's hair, and mine in particular, had regrown curiously smooth and soft; at that time my hair was still very short, and Cesare maintained that it reminded him of a rabbit's skin. Now 'rabbit', or rather 'rabbit skin', in the merchant's jargon which Cesare knew well, is called Lapè. Daniele, on the other hand, the bearded, hirsute heavy-browed Daniele, as ardent for vengeance and justice as a prophet of old, was called Coralli; because, said Cesare, if corallines (glass beads) were to rain down, they would all be spiked in his hair.

'Bravo, Lapè,' he said to me; and then he explained his plan. Cesare in fact, was a man of crazy designs, which he then pursued with much practical sense. He had not dreamt up the chicken; he had seen a well-beaten, and hence recent, path leading north from the hut. It probably led to a village; and if there was a village, there were also chickens. He went out into the open; it was now almost dark, and Cesare was right. On the brow of a barely perceptible rise in the ground, perhaps a mile and a half away, we could see a light shining between the tree trunks. So we left, stumbling over roots, pursued by swarms of voracious mosquitoes; we were carrying with us the only commodity our group had finally agreed to part with: our six plates, ordinary earthenware plates which the Russians had previously distributed as our equipment.

We walked in the dark, taking care not to lose the path, and shouting at intervals. No-one replied in the village. When we were about a hundred yards away, Cesare stopped, drew in his breath and shouted: 'Hi! Russkies! We are friends. Italiansky. Have you got a chicken to sell?' This time the reply came: a flash in the dark, a sharp crack, and the whistling of a bullet, some feet above our heads. I flattened myself on the ground, cautiously so as not to break the plates; but Cesare was furious, and stayed on his feet: 'Blast you! We're friends, I told you! We're as straight as they come – see for yourselves. We only want a chicken. We're not bandits, we're not Deutschky; we are Italiansky!'

There were no further shots, and already we could see human profiles on the brow of the hill. We approached cautiously, Cesare first, continuing his persuasive speech, and I behind, ready to throw myself on the ground a second time.

Finally we reached the village. There were no more than five or six wooden houses grouped around a minute square, and on the square, waiting for us, stood the entire population, about thirty people, for the most part old women, then children and dogs, all visibly alarmed. From the little crowd a grand bearded old man emerged, the one who had fired; he still held the firearm in his hand.

Cesare now considered that he had done his part, the strategic part, and called on me to do my duty. 'Now it's your turn. What are you waiting for? Explain to him that we are Italians, that we don't want to harm anybody, and that we want to buy a chicken to roast.'

The people were considering us with diffident curiosity. They seemed satisfied that, although dressed like two convicts, we could not be dangerous. The old women had stopped cackling, and the dogs had also quietened down. The old man with the gun asked us questions which we did not understand; I knew only about a hundred words of Russian, and none of these was suited to the situation, except for *'Italiansky'*. So I repeated *'Italiansky'* frequently, until the old man in his turn began to say *'Italiansky'* for the benefit of the bystanders.

In the meantime Cesare, more down to earth, had taken the plates out of the sack, had placed five of them well in view on the ground as if at the market, and held the sixth in his hand, tapping it on the edge with his nail to show it gave the right sound. The peasant women looked on, amused and curious. *'Tarelki,'* said one. *'Tarelki, da!'* I replied, delighted at learning the name of the merchandise we were offering; at which one of them stretched a hesitant hand towards the plate which Cesare was displaying. 'Hey there, what do you take me for?' he said, withdrawing it quickly: 'We're not giving them away!' And he turned to me waspishly: Well,

138

what was I waiting for? Why didn't I ask for the chicken in exchange? What use were all my studies?

I was in a pickle. Russian, they say, is an Indo-European language, and chickens must have been known to our common ancestors in an epoch certainly previous to their subdivision into the various modern ethnic families. '*His fretus,*' that is to say, on these fine foundations, I tried to say 'chicken' and 'bird' in all the ways known to me, but without any visible result.

Cesare was also perplexed. Cesare, deep down, had never really accepted that Germans speak German, and Russians Russian, except out of gross malice; then, in his heart of hearts, he was persuaded that they only pretended not to understand Italian through some refinement of the same malice. Malice, or extreme and scandalous ignorance: clear barbarism. There could be no other explanation. So his perplexity rapidly changed to anger.

He grumbled and swore. Was it possible that it was so difficult to understand what a chicken is, and that we wanted it in exchange for six plates? A chicken, one of those beasts that go around pecking, scratching and saying 'coccode-e-eh'; and rather half-heartedly, glowering and sullen, he put on a very second-rate imitation of the habits of the chicken, crouching on the ground, scraping first with one foot and then with the other, and pecking here and there with his hand shaped like a wedge. Between one oath and the other, he also cried 'coccode-e-eh'; but this rendering of the chicken's cry is of course highly conventional; it is only to be heard in Italy and has no currency elsewhere.

So the result was negative. They goggled at us with amazement, and certainly took us for madmen. Why, for what conceivable reason, had we come from the ends of the earth to play the fool on their square? Hopping mad by now, Cesare even tried to lay an egg, pouring far-fetched insults on them all the while, so rendering the meaning of his performance even more obscure. At this improper spectacle, the house-wives' chattering rose by an octave, and turned into the buzz of a disturbed wasps' nest.

When I noticed one of the old women approaching the old man, and speaking to him, looking nervously at us mean-while, I realized that the situation was getting out of hand. I made Cesare get out of his unnatural posture, calmed him and approached the man together with him. 'Excuse me,' I said to the man and led him near a window, where a lamp lit up a piece of ground quite well. Here, painfully aware of the many suspicious glances, I drew a chicken on the ground, complete in all its attributes, including an egg behind it, to avoid all ambiguity.

Then I got up and said: 'You – plates. We – eat.'

A brief consultation followed; then an old woman sprang out of the hut, her eyes alight with joy and comprehension; she stepped forward a couple of paces, and in a shrill voice pronounced: '*Kura! Kuritsa!*'

She was very proud and happy that she had been the one to resolve the enigma. From all sides laughter and applause broke out and voices cried '*Kuritsa, Kuritsa!*'; and we also clapped our hands, caught up in the game and in the general enthusiasm. The old woman curtsied, like an actress at the end of her performance; she disappeared and re-emerged after a few minutes holding a hen already plucked. She dangled it comically under Cesare's nose, as a double check; and when she saw that he reacted positively, she loosened her hold, collected the plates and carried them off.

Cesare, who understood these matters because he had once had a stall at Porta Portese market, assured me that the '*kurizetta*', the little hen, was fat enough, and worth our six plates. We took it back to the hut, woke up our companions who had already fallen asleep, relit the fire, cooked the chicken and ate it with our fingers because we no longer had any plates.

11. Old Roads

THE HEN, AND the night spent in the open, were as good as a medicine for us. After a sound sleep, which wholly revived us, although we had slept on the bare ground, we woke up in the morning in excellent humour and health. We were contented, because of the sun, because we felt free, because of the good smell coming from the earth, and also a little because a couple of miles away there were people not hostile to us, in fact cheerful and ready to laugh; it was true that they had shot at us, but they had afterwards welcomed us and had even sold us a chicken. We were contented because that day (we did not know about the next; but what happens tomorrow is not always important) we could do things which we had not done for too long; drink water from a well, stretch out in the sun in the middle of tall robust grass, smell the summer air, light a fire and cook, go into the woods in search of strawberries and mushrooms, smoke a cigarette looking at the high sky swept clean by the wind.

We could do these things and we did them, with puerile joy. But our resources were coming to an end; we could not live on strawberries and mushrooms, and none of us (not even Cesare, a townsman and Roman citizen 'since Nero's time') was morally and technically equipped for a precarious life of vagabondage and rural thefts. The choice was clear: either to rejoin at once the ranks of civilization, or to go hungry. Twenty miles of a dizzily straight road, however, still separated us from civilization, represented by the mysterious camp of Starye Dorogi. If we managed to cover them in one go, perhaps we should arrive in time for the evening meal; otherwise, we should have to camp once more on the road, in liberty, but on an empty stomach.

A rapid census of our possessions was carried out. They were not much; eight rubles in all. It was difficult to calculate their purchasing power, at that moment and in that place; our previous monetary experiences with the Russians had been incoherent and absurd. Some of them accepted money from any country without difficulty, even German or Polish money; others were suspicious, afraid of being cheated, and only accepted exchanges in kind or in metal coinage. Indeed the most improbable coinage was circulating: coins from Tsarist times, brought out of ancestral hiding places; guineas, Scandinavian crowns, even old coins of the Austro-Hungarian Empire. In contrast, at Zhmerinka we had seen the walls of one of the station latrines studded with German marks, meticulously stuck on to the wall one by one with an unmentionable material.

In any case, eight rubles were not much; the price of one or two eggs. It was decided corporately that Cesare and I, now accredited as ambassadors, should go back to the village, and see on the spot what could best be bought with eight rubles.

We set off, and as we walked an idea occurred to us; not goods, but services. The best investment would be to ask our friends for the hire of a horse and cart as far as Starye Dorogi. Perhaps the money was too little, but we could try offering an item of clothing: it was hot enough anyway. So we arrived at the square, welcomed by friendly greetings and sly understanding smiles from the old women, and furious barks from the dogs. When silence had been re-established, remembering my Michael Strogov and other books read long ago, I said: *'Telega. Starye Dorogi,'* and showed my eight rubles.

A confused murmuring followed: strange to say, no-one had understood. Nevertheless, my task looked like being less arduous than it had been on the previous evening; in a corner of the yard, under a roof, I had seen a four-wheeled farm cart, long and narrow, with sides like a 'V'; in short, a telega. I touched it, a little impatient at the obtuseness of these people: was this not a telega?

'*Tyelyega!*' the old man corrected me, with paternal severity, scandalized at my barbaric pronunciation.

'*Da. Tyelyega na Starye Dorogi.* We pay. Eight rubles.'

The offer was derisory: the equivalent of two eggs against twenty plus twenty miles of road, twelve hours' travel. Instead, the old man pocketed the rubles, disappeared into the stable, returned with a mule, harnessed it, signed to us to climb on, loaded a few sacks, still in silence, and drove off towards the main road. Cesare went to call the others, in front of whom we naturally showed off like peacocks. We were to enjoy an extremely comfortable journey in a *telega* or rather in a *tyelyega*, and a triumphal entry at Starye Dorogi, all for eight rubles; that is what a knowledge of languages and diplomatic ability means.

In reality, we soon realized (so, unfortunately, did our companions) that the eight rubles had been virtually wasted: the old man had to go to Starye Dorogi in any case, on some business of his own, and would perhaps even have taken us free of charge.

We set out about midday, lying down on the old man's not very soft sacks. However, it was still much better than travelling on foot; we could also enjoy the countryside in comfort.

For us the countryside was unusual and stupendous. The plain, which the day before had oppressed us with its solemn emptiness, was no longer rigorously flat. It rippled in light, barely perceptible undulations, perhaps the remains of ancient dunes, not more than a few feet high, but enough to break the monotony, rest the eyes, and create a rhythm, a measure. Pools and marshes, large and small, stretched between one undulation and the next. The open ground was

143

sandy, and here and there bristled with wild clumps of shrubs; elsewhere there were tall trees, but these were few and isolated. On both sides of the road lay shapeless rusty relics, guns, tanks, barbed wire, helmets, drums; the remnants of two armies which had confronted each other in these parts for so many months. We had entered the region of the Pripet marshes.

The road and countryside were deserted, but a little before dusk we noticed that someone was coming after us: a man, black against the white of the dust, was walking vigorously in our direction. Slowly but steadily he gained ground; soon he was within hailing distance, and we recognized the Moor, Avesani of Avesa, the grand old man. He too had spent the night in some hiding place, and was now striding towards Starye Dorogi with the impetus of a tempest, his white hair in the wind, his bloodshot eyes staring ahead of him. He moved forward regularly and powerfully like a steam locomotive; he had tied his famous, weighty bundle on his back and hanging from this his axe flashed, like the Scythe of Kronos.

He prepared to pass us as if he had not seen us or did not recognize us. Cesare called to him and invited him to climb on with us. 'Desecration of the world! Dirty inhuman swine!' the Moor replied promptly, giving voice to the blasphemous litany which perpetually filled his mind. He overtook us, and continued his epic march towards the horizon opposite.

Mr Unverdorben knew much more than we did about the Moor; we now learnt from him that the Moor was not (or was not only) an old lunatic. The bundle had its reason, as did the old man's wandering life. A widower for many years, he had a daughter, only one, now almost fifty, and paralysed in bed; she would never recover. The Moor lived for his daughter; every week he wrote her letters destined never to reach her; for her alone he had worked all his life, and had turned as dark as oak and as hard as stone. For her alone, wandering

around the world as a migrant, the Moor pocketed everything that came his way, any object that presented even the
smallest potentiality for use or for exchange.

We met no other living creature until we came to Starye
Dorogi.

Starye Dorogi was a surprise. It was not a village; or
rather, there was a minute village, in the middle of the wood,
a little way off the road; but we learnt about this later, as we
also learnt that its name meant 'Old Roads'. The canton-
ment assigned to us fourteen hundred Italians, however, was
a single gigantic building, isolated on the edge of the road in
the middle of uncultivated fields, on the fringe of the forest.
Its name was 'Krasny Dom', the Red House, and in fact it
was unstintingly red, both inside and out.

It was a truly singular building, which had grown without
order in all directions like a volcanic flow; it was difficult to
tell whether it was the work of many architects at loggerheads,
or of a single one who was mad. The nucleus, now overwhelmed and suffocated by wings and extensions added confusedly later on, consisted of a three-storey block divided into
small rooms, perhaps formerly used as military or administrative offices. But around this kernel there was everything:
a room for lectures or meetings, a series of classrooms,
kitchens, washrooms, a theatre to seat at least a thousand, a
surgery, a gymnasium; and next to the main door, a little
storeroom with mysterious brackets, which we took to be a
ski deposit. But here too, as at Slutsk, nothing or almost
nothing remained of the furniture and fittings; not only was
there no water, but even the pipes had been carried away, as
had the kitchen stoves, the theatre seats, the classroom
benches, the banisters of the staircases. The most obsessive
feature of the Red House was its staircases. They were to be
found in abundance in the interminable building: emphatic
and prolix staircases leading to absurd attics full of dust and
rubbish; other narrow irregular staircases, blocked half-way

by a column heaved up amateurishly to support a collapsing ceiling; fragments of warped, forked, anomalous staircases, linking floors of different levels in adjacent buildings. Memorable even among all these, along one of the façades ran a Cyclopean staircase, which climbed fifty feet up from a grass-covered courtyard, by steps three yards wide, and led nowhere.

Around the Red House there was no fence, not even a symbolical one as at Katowice. Nor were we under any regularly constituted surveillance; at the entrance there was often a Russian soldier, usually a boy, but he had no instructions about us Italians. His duty was solely to prevent other Russians coming at night to molest the Italian women in their quarters.

The Russians, officers and soldiers, lived in a wooden hut nearby, and other Russians, in transit along the road, occasionally stopped there; but they rarely bothered about us. The people who did bother about us were a small group of Italian officers, ex-prisoners of war, somewhat arrogant and uncivil; they were heavily conscious of their status as soldiers, they showed contempt and indifference towards us civilians, and – which somewhat surprised us – they maintained excellent relations with their Soviet counterparts in the hut next door. In fact, they enjoyed a privileged position not only in comparison with us, but also in comparison with the Soviet soldiers; they ate in the Russian officers' mess, they were given new Soviet uniforms (without badges of rank) and good military boots, and slept in camp beds with sheets and blankets.

Not, however, that the rest of us had any reason to complain. We were treated exactly like the Russian soldiers as regards food and lodgings, and were not subjected to any particular regulations or discipline. Only a few Italians worked and these had offered spontaneously to run the kitchens, the baths and the generating plant. In addition,

Leonardo acted as a doctor, and I as a nurse; but now, with the good weather, there were very few patients, and our offices were sinecures.

Anyone who wanted to could leave. Several did so, some from sheer boredom or from a spirit of adventure, others in an attempt to pass the frontiers and return to Italy; but they all returned, after a few weeks or months of vagabondage; for, although the camp was neither guarded nor fenced, the distant frontiers were, and strongly so.

On the Russian side there were no attempts to exert ideological pressure, in fact, no attempt to discriminate between us. Our community was too complicated; whether we were ex-soldiers of the ARMIR, ex-partisans, ex-Häftlinge from Auschwitz, ex-workers from the Todt Organization, ex-criminals or prostitutes from Milan jail, Communists, Monarchists or Fascists, the Russians displayed the most impartial indifference towards us. We were Italians, and that was enough; the rest was 'vsyo ravno', all the same.

We slept on wooden planks covered with straw sacks: two feet per man. At first we protested, because it seemed too little, but the Russian Command pointed out courteously that our complaint was unfounded. At the head of the planks, scribbled in pencil, we could still read the names of Soviet soldiers who had occupied these places before us; we could judge for ourselves – there was one name per eighteen inches.

The same could be said, and was, about the food. We received two pounds of bread a day: rye bread, scarcely leavened, damp and sour; but it was a large ration and it was their bread. And the daily 'kasha' was their 'kasha': a compact block of lard, millet, beans, meat and spices, nourishing but ferociously indigestible, which we only learnt to render edible after several days of experiments by boiling it for some hours.

Three or four times a week, fish, 'ribba', was also distributed. It was river fish, of doubtful freshness, full of bones, heavy, raw, unsalted. What could we do with it? Few of us were ready to eat it as it was (as did many Russians); to cook it, we needed pots, seasoning, salt and skill. We soon concluded that the best thing was to sell it to the Russians themselves, to peasants at the village or to soldiers passing along the road; a new business for Cesare, who in a short time carried it to a high degree of technical perfection.

On the morning of the fish days, Cesare went around the dormitories, carrying a piece of wire. He collected the *'ribba'*, stuck the wire through its eyes, slung the stinking garland round his shoulders and disappeared. He returned after many hours, sometimes not until the evening, and distributed equitably among his contractors rubles, cheese, quarters of chickens and eggs, to everybody's advantage, and above all to his own.

With the first profits of his trade he bought a balance, which noticeably increased his professional prestige. But to put a plan of his into effect he also needed another instrument of less obvious utility: a syringe. There was no hope of finding one at the Russian village, and so he came to me in the surgery, and asked if I could lend him one.

'What do you want to do with it?' I asked him.

'It's none of your business. I want a syringe; you have plenty here.'

'What size?'

'The biggest you have. It doesn't matter even if it's a little the worse for wear.'

In fact there was one, with a capacity of one fluid ounce, cracked and practically useless. Cesare examined it with care, and declared that it was what he needed.

'But what are you going to do with it?' I asked again. Cesare looked at me sullenly, hurt by my lack of tact. He told me that it was his affair, his own bloody business, an experiment which might end well or badly, and that in any case I was a fine friend sticking my nose into what had nothing to do with me. He wrapped up the syringe carefully and went off like an offended prince.

However, the secret of the syringe did not last long: life at Starye Dorogi was too idle for gossip and curiosity not to proliferate. In the following days, Cesare was seen by Signora Letizia going to fetch water in a bucket and carrying it to the woods; he was seen by Stellina in the woods, sitting on the ground with the bucket in the middle of a garland of fish, which 'he seemed to be feeding'; and finally he was met in the village by Rovati, his rival: he was without his bucket and selling fish, but they were strange fish, fat, firm and round, and not flat and limp like those we were given.

As happens with many scientific discoveries, the idea of the syringe had originated in a failure and in a fortuitous observation. A few days before, Cesare had exchanged fish at the village for a live chicken. He had returned to the Red House convinced that he had struck a good bargain; in return for only two fish they had given him a fine chicken, admittedly not young and with rather a melancholic air, but extraordinarily large and plump. Only after he had killed and plucked it had he realized that something was wrong; the chicken was unsymmetrical: its stomach was all on one side, and to touch it gave an impression of something hard, mobile and elastic. It was not the egg: it was a large watery cyst.

Naturally Cesare had to recoup his losses: he had managed to sell the animal immediately to no less a person than Mr Rovi, and had even made a profit; but then, like a Stendhalian hero, he had thought about it. Why not imitate nature? Why not try with the fish?

At first he had tried to fill them with water through their mouths by means of a tube, but the water all poured out again. Then he had thought of the syringe. With the syringe he noted a certain progress in many cases, but this was clearly dependent on the point at which the injection was made:

sometimes the water came out again, immediately or soon after, at other times it stayed in indefinitely. Cesare had then dissected several fish with a knife, and managed to ascertain that, for a permanent effect, the injection needed to be made in the swimming bladder.

As a result the fish, which Cesare sold by weight, yielded from twenty to thirty per cent more than normal, besides having a far more attractive appearance. Certainly, the 'ribba' treated like this could not be sold twice to the same client; but it could be sold extremely well to demobilized Russian soldiers passing along the road towards the East, who would only discover the trick some miles farther on.

But one day Cesare returned black in the face; he was without fish, money or goods: 'I've been bamboozled.' For two days it was impossible to speak to him; he lay on the straw hunched up, as bristly as a porcupine, and only came down for meals. Things had not gone as usual.

He recounted his adventure to me much later, one long warm evening, making me swear not to spread it around, because, if it was known, his commercial honour would suffer. In fact, the fish had not been torn from him violently by a furious Russian, as at first he had tried to pretend; the truth was quite different. He had given the fish away, he confessed to me, full of shame.

He had gone to the village, and, to avoid clients who had already been had, he kept off the main road and took a path leading through the woods; after a few hundred yards he saw an isolated cottage, or rather a ramshackle hut built of un-cemented bricks and corrugated iron. A skinny woman dressed in black and three pale children were sitting on the threshold. He approached, and offered her the fish, and she made him understand that she would have liked the fish, but had nothing to give him in exchange; in fact, she and the children had not eaten for two days. She also made him enter the hut, and there was nothing inside, only piles of straw as in a kennel.

At this point the children had looked at him with such eyes that Cesare had thrown down the fish and run away like a thief.

12. The Wood and the Path

WE STAYED AT Starye Dorogi, in that Red House full of mystery and pitfalls like a fairy castle, for two long months: from 15th July to 15th September 1945.

They were months of idleness and relative comfort, and full, therefore, of a penetrating nostalgia. Nostalgia is a fragile and tender anguish, basically different, more intimate, more human than the other pains we had endured till then – beatings, cold, hunger, terror, destitution, disease. Nostalgia is a limpid and clean pain, but demanding; it permeates every minute of the day, permits no other thoughts, and induces a need for escape.

Perhaps because of this, the forest around the camp exercised a deep attraction upon us. Perhaps because it offered the inestimable gift of solitude to all who sought it; we had been deprived of this for so long! Perhaps because it reminded us of other woods, other solitudes of our previous existence; or perhaps, on the other hand, because it was solemn and austere and untouched like no other scenery known to us.

To the north of the Red House, beyond the road, there was a varied zone of thickets, glades and pine woods, broken by marshes and strips of fine white sand; you came across winding, barely discernible paths, leading to distant farms. But to the south, only a few hundred yards from the Red House, every human trace disappeared. So did every sign of animal life, except for the occasional fawn-coloured flash of a squirrel, or the sinister steady eye of a water snake, wrapped round a rotting trunk. There were no paths, no traces of woodsmen, nothing: only silence, desolation and tree trunks in all directions, pale birches, red-brown conifers, shooting vertically towards the invisible sky; the ground was equally invisible, covered by a thick layer of dead leaves and pine needles, and by clumps of wild waist-high undergrowth.

The first time I penetrated it, I learnt to my cost, with surprise and fear, that the risk of 'losing oneself in a wood' existed not only in fairy tales. I had been walking for about an hour, orientating myself as best I could by the sun, which was visible occasionally, where the branches were less thick; but then the sky clouded over, threatening rain, and when I wanted to return I realized that I had lost the north. Moss on the tree trunks? It covered them on all sides. I set out in what seemed the correct direction; but after a long and painful walk through the brambles and undergrowth I found myself in as unrecognizable a spot as that from which I had started.

I walked on for hours, increasingly tired and uneasy, almost until dusk; and I was already beginning to think that even if my companions came to search for me, they would not find me, or would only find me days later, exhausted by hunger, perhaps already dead. As daylight began to fade, swarms of large hungry mosquitoes rose up, as well as other unclassifiable insects, as large and hard as bullets, which darted blindly among the tree trunks, smashing into my face. Then I decided to set off straight ahead, generally speaking towards the north (that is, leaving on my left a slightly more luminous bit of sky, which should have corresponded to the west), and to walk without stopping until I met the main road, or in any case a path or a track. So I continued in the prolonged twilight of the northern summer, until it was almost night, a prey now to utter panic, to the age-old fear of the dark, the forest and the unknown. Despite my weariness, I felt a violent impulse to rush headlong in any direction, and to continue running so long as my strength and breath lasted.

Suddenly I heard the whistle of a train: this meant the railway was to my right, when, according to my calculations, it should have been far away to the left. So I had been going in the wrong direction. Following the noise of the train, I arrived at the railway before nightfall; then I kept to the glinting railway lines, moving in the direction of the Little Bear which had reappeared amid the clouds, and reached safety, first at Starye Dorogi, then at the Red House.

But there were some who had moved to the forest, and lived there: the first had been Cantarella, one of the 'Rumanians', who had discovered his vocation as a hermit. Cantarella was a Calabrian sailor, tall and ascetically thin, taciturn and misanthropic. He had built a hut from tree trunks and branches, half an hour's walk from the camp, and here he lived in wild solitude, dressed only in a loin-cloth. He was a contemplative, but not an idler; he exercised a curious priestly activity.

He possessed a hammer and a sort of roughly cast anvil, which he had salvaged from some war scrap and fixed in a tree stump; with these tools, and with empty food tins, he produced pots and pans with great skill and religious diligence.

He produced them on order, for the new couples. When, in our heterogeneous community, a man and woman decided to live together, and hence felt the need for a minimum of utensils to set up house, they went to Cantarella, holding hands. Without asking questions, he set to work, and in little more than an hour, with expert blows of the hammer, bent and twisted the tinplate into the forms that the couple desired. He did not ask for payment, but accepted gifts in kind, such as bread, cheese, eggs. In this manner, the marriage was celebrated, and in this manner Cantarella lived.

There were also other inhabitants of the wood; I realized this one day, when I chanced across a path that ran westwards, straight and clearly visible, which previously I had not noticed. It led to a particularly thick region of the wood, where it threaded its way along an old trench, and ended at the entrance to a casemate of trunks, almost totally underground: only the roof and the chimney projected above the surface. I pushed at the door, which yielded; there was nobody inside but the place was clearly inhabited. On the bare soil forming the floor (which was swept and clean) there was a stove, plates, an army bowl; in the corner, a pile of hay; hung on the walls, feminine clothing and photographs of men.

I returned to the camp, and discovered that I was the only one not to know about it: it was common knowledge that two German women lived in the casemate. They were two auxiliaries of the Wehrmacht, who had not managed to follow the Germans in defeat, and had remained isolated in the Russian wastes. They were afraid of the Russians, and had not given themselves up; for months they had lived precariously, by small thefts, by gathering herbs, and by occasional furtive prostitution to Englishmen and Frenchmen who had occupied the Red House before us – until the arrival of the Italians had brought them prosperity and safety.

In our colony, women were few, not more than two hundred, and almost all had soon reached a stable arrangement: they were no longer available. So, to go to 'the girls in the wood' had become a habit for an indefinite number of Italians, and the only alternative to celibacy. An alternative which was rich with a complex fascination; because the matter was secret and vaguely dangerous (much more for the women than for them); because the girls were foreigners and had grown half savage; because they were in need, and so gave one the ennobling feeling of 'protecting' them; and because of the exotic, fairy-tale scenery of the meetings.

Not only Cantarella, but the Velletrano as well had found his personality in the woods. The experiment of transplanting a 'savage' into civilization has been tried many times, often with excellent results, to demonstrate the fundamental unity of the human species; with the Velletrano the opposite was

155

accomplished, for, a native of the Jewish quarter of Rome, he had been transformed back into a 'savage' with admirable ease.

In fact, he could never have been very civilized. The Velletrano was a Jew of about thirty, a survivor of Auschwitz. He must have created a problem for the Lager official responsible for tattoos, because both his muscular forearms were already thickly covered with them: Cesare, who had known him for some time, explained to me that they were the names of his women; he also pointed out that the Velletrano's real name was not Velletrano, nor had he been born at Velletri, but had been sent out there to wet-nurse.

He rarely spent the night at the Red House; he lived in the forest, barefoot and half naked. He lived like our progenitors; he laid traps for hares and foxes, climbed up trees after nests, brought down turtle doves with stones, and was not above raiding the chicken runs of the most distant farms; he collected mushrooms and berries generally held to be inedible, and in the evening one often met him near the camp, crouching on his heels in front of a large fire, roasting the day's prey and singing uncouthly. Afterwards, he would go to sleep on the bare ground, lying near the embers. But, as he was still born of man, in his own way he pursued virtue and knowledge, and day by day perfected his art and his instruments; he fabricated a knife, then a spear and an axe, and had he had the time, without doubt he would have rediscovered agriculture and pasturage.

When he had had a good day, he became sociable and affable; through Cesare, who willingly presented him like a freak at a fair, and who recounted his earlier legendary adventures, he invited everybody to Homeric feasts of roast meats; if anyone refused, he turned nasty and pulled out his knife.

After a few days of rain, followed by sun and wind, the mushrooms and bilberries in the wood grew with such abundance as to become of interest no longer from a purely bucolic or sporting point of view, but from a strictly utilitarian one. After taking appropriate measures to avoid losing the way, everybody spent whole days collecting them. The bilberries, which grew in much taller thickets than in Mediterranean countries, were almost as large as nuts, and very tasty; we took them back to camp by the pound, and even tried (in vain) to ferment their juice into wine. As for the mushrooms, there were two varieties: there were the normal brown mushrooms, savoury and certainly edible; and another type, similar to the former in shape and smell, but larger and tougher with slightly different colours.

None of us was certain if these latter were edible; on the other hand, could they be left to rot in the wood? They could not: we were all badly under-nourished, and, even more important, our memory of the hunger of Auschwitz was still too recent, and had changed into a violent mental stimulus, which obliged us to fill our stomachs to the utmost and imperiously forbade us to renounce any opportunity of eating. Cesare collected a fair quantity, and boiled them according to a recipe unknown to me, adding to the stew vodka and garlic bought in the village, because they 'kill all poisons'. Then he himself ate some, not much, and offered a little to many of us, so as to limit the risk and collect abundant evidence for the day after. The following day he walked around the dormitories and had never been so polite and solicitous: 'How are you, Signora Elvira? How are you, Don Vincenzo? Did you sleep well? Did you have a good night?' And meanwhile he examined their faces with a clinical eye. They were all well, the strange mushrooms could be eaten.

For the laziest and richest, there was no need to go to the wood to find extra provisions. Commercial contacts between the village of Starye Dorogi and the occupants of the Red House had soon become intensive. Every day peasant women arrived with baskets and pails; they sat on the ground, and stayed there for hours, without moving, waiting for clients. If a rain cloud burst, they did not leave, but merely pulled their skirts over their heads. Two or three times the Russians tried to drive them away, and stuck up bilingual edicts, which threatened both parties with punishments of crazy severity; then, as normally occurred, they lost interest in the matter, and the exchanges continued undisturbed.

There were old and young peasant women; the former were dressed in the traditional manner, with quilted blouses and skirts and handkerchiefs tied over their heads; the latter, in light cotton garments, went about for the most part barefoot and were frank, bold and ready to laugh, but not brazen. In addition to mushrooms, bilberries and raspberries, they sold milk, cheese, eggs, chickens, lettuce and fruit, and in exchange accepted fish, bread, tobacco and any piece of clothing or fabric, however torn and threadbare; naturally rubles could be used by those who still possessed them.

In a short time Cesare knew all the women, especially the young ones. I often went with him to these peasants, to listen to their interesting bargaining. I do not intend to deny the utility of speaking the same language in business affairs, but I can affirm from experience that it is not strictly necessary; each of the two knows exactly what the other wants, and although initially he does not know the intensity of the desire to buy or sell respectively, he can deduce it with excellent approximation from the expression on the other's face, from his gestures and from the number of his replies.

Let us look at Cesare, who is going to the market early in the morning with a fish. He looks for and finds Irina, his friend, his contemporary, whose sympathies he has conquered some time before by baptizing her 'Greta Garbo' and giving her a pencil; Irina has a cow and sells milk, *moloko*; in fact, in the evening, returning from the pasturage, she often stops in front of the Red House and milks the cow directly into her clients' receptacles. The problem today is to agree how much milk Cesare's fish is worth; Cesare is carrying a half-gallon pail (it is one of Cantarella's, which Cesare had picked up cheaply from a '*ménage*' which had broken down through incompatibility), and with his hand flat, palm down, indicates that he wants it full. Irina laughs, and replies with quick harmonious words, probably insults; she slaps away Cesare's hand, and with two fingers points half-way up the side of the pail.

Now it is Cesare's turn to grow angry; he brandishes the fish ('untreated'), dangles it in the air by its tail with an enormous effort, as if it weighed a hundredweight, and says: 'Look at the size!', then runs its entire length under Irina's nose, and while doing this closes his eyes and draws in his breath deeply, as if inebriated with the fragrance of the fish. Irina takes advantage of the second in which Cesare's eyes are closed to snatch the fish from him as quickly as a cat, to bite off its head cleanly with her white teeth, and to slap the flaccid mutilated corpse in Cesare's face, with all her considerable strength. Then, so as not to ruin their friendship and the bargaining, she touches the pail at the three-quarter mark: three pints. Half stunned by the blow, Cesare mutters a string of obscene gallantries which he judges fit to restore his virile honour; then, however, he accepts Irina's last offer, and leaves her the fish, which she devours on the spot.

We were to meet the voracious Irina later, several times, in a context which to us Latins seemed somewhat embarrassing, but which was perfectly natural to her.

In a glade in the wood, halfway between the village and the camp, was the public bath, to be found in every Russian village, and which at Starye Dorogi functioned on alternate days for the Russians and for us. It was a wooden hut, with two long stone benches inside, and zinc wash tubs of various sizes scattered about. On the wall there were taps with abundant hot and cold water. The soap, on the other hand, was not abundant: it was distributed with great parsimony in the dressing-room. The official responsible for the distribution of the soap was Irina.

She sat at a table with a small block of smelly greyish soap on it, and held a knife in her hand. We undressed, handed in our clothes for disinfection, and lined up completely nude in front of Irina's table. The girl was extremely serious and incorruptible when carrying out her duties as a public official; she frowned with attention and stuck her tongue between her teeth like a child, as she cut a small slice of soap for everyone aspiring to a bath; a little thinner for skinny people, a little thicker for fat people, either because she had been ordered to do so, or because she was moved by an unconscious desire for a just distribution. Not a muscle of her face moved at the impertinences of her more foul-mouthed customers.

After the bath, we had to recover our clothes from the disinfection room; this was another surprise of the Starye Dorogi régime. The room was heated at 250° Fahrenheit: the first time they told us we had to enter it personally to get our clothing, we looked at each other, perplexed; Russians are made of iron, as we had seen many times, but we were not, and we should certainly be roasted. Then someone tried, and we saw that the exploit was not so terrible as it seemed, so long as one observed the following precautions: to enter while still wet; to know the number of one's hanger in advance; to take a deep breath before passing through the door and then not to breathe again and not to touch any metal object; above all, to hurry.

The disinfected clothing presented interesting phenomena; corpses of exploded lice, strangely deformed; plastic pens, forgotten in a pocket by some plutocrat, distorted and with the cover sealed up; melted candle ends soaked up by the cloth; an egg, left in a pocket as an experiment, cracked open and dried out into a horny mass, but still edible. But the two Russian attendants walked in and out of the furnace with indifference, like the legendary salamander.

So the days at Starye Dorogi passed by, in an interminable indolence, as sleepy and salubrious as a long holiday, only broken at intervals by the painful thought of a distant home and by the enchantment of our rediscovery of nature. It was useless to go to the Russians of the Command to ask why we were not returning, when we should return, by what road, what future awaited us; they knew no more than we did, or else, with polite candour, they proffered fantastic or terrifying or senseless answers: that there were no trains; or that war against America was about to start; that soon we should be sent to work in the *kolkhoz*; that they were waiting to exchange us for Russian prisoners in Italy. They told us these and other enormities without hatred or derision, in fact with an almost affectionate solicitude, as if they were speaking to children who asked too many questions, to quieten them.

They simply could not understand our haste to return home: were we not given food and beds? What did we lack at Starye Dorogi? We did not even have to work; did they, soldiers of the Red Army, who had fought four years, and had won the war, complain about not being sent home?

In fact they were returning home haphazardly, slowly and, to judge from appearances, in extreme disorder. The spectacle of the Russian demobilization, which we had already admired at the station of Katowice, now continued in a different form before our eyes, day by day; groups of the victorious army passed by, no longer by rail, but along the road in front of the Red House, moving from west to east, in tight or straggling bands, at all hours of the day and night. Men passed by on foot, often barefoot, with their shoes hanging from their shoulders to save the soles, because the march was long; with or without uniforms, armed or un-armed, some singing lustily, others grey-faced and exhausted. Some carried sacks or suitcases on their shoulders; others, the most varied of possessions, an easy chair, a standard lamp, copper pots, a radio, a pendulum clock.

Others passed by on carts, or on horseback; yet others, droves of them, on motor-cycles, driven at intoxicating speed, with an infernal noise. American Dodge trucks passed by, packed with men clinging even to the bonnet and mud-guards; other trucks were towing equally packed trailers. We saw one of these trailers travelling on three wheels; a pine-trunk had been fixed as well as possible in place of the fourth wheel at an angle, so that one extremity rested and dragged along the ground. As it was slowly consumed by friction, the tree-trunk was pushed gradually farther down, so as to main-tain the vehicle's equilibrium. Almost in front of the Red House one of the three remaining tyres deflated; the occu-pants, about twenty, got down, overturned the trailer to clear the road and again packed into the already overloaded truck, which left in a cloud of dust, while everybody cheered.

Other unusual vehicles also passed, always crammed: agricultural tractors, postal vans, German buses formerly used for city transport and still bearing the names of the Berlin terminals; some already broken down, and dragged by other vehicles or by horses.

About the beginning of August, this multiple migration imperceptibly changed character. Horses slowly began to prevail over vehicles; after a week, one could only see the former, the road belonged to them. There must have been all the horses of occupied Germany, tens of thousands passing through each day; they moved by endlessly, tired, sweating, starving, accompanied by clouds of horse-flies and by sharp animal smells; they were goaded and urged on with cries and blows of the whip by girls, one to every hundred or more animals, who rode on horseback, without a saddle, bare-legged, sunburnt and dishevelled. In the evening, they drove the horses off the road into the fields and woods, so that they could graze in liberty and rest till dawn. There were carthorses, thoroughbreds, mules, mares with foals still sucking, rheumatic old hacks, asses; we soon realized not only that they were not counted, but also that their drovers took no interest at all in the animals which dropped out because they were tired or ill or limping, or in those which were lost during the night. The horses were so many, what did it matter if one more or less reached its destination?

But for us, almost wholly deprived of meat for eighteen months, one horse more or less could make all the difference. The person to begin the hunt was, naturally, the Velletrano; he came to wake us one morning, covered in blood from head to foot, still clasping the primordial tool he had used, a splinter of an artillery shell tied with leather thongs to a forked stick.

From the investigation we carried out (because the Velletrano was not very good at explaining himself in words) it emerged that he had given the *coup de grâce* to a horse probably already on its last legs; the poor animal had a highly equivocal look, its stomach so swollen that it sounded like a drum, and froth on its mouth; it must have been kicking all night, as it lay on its side in its death agony, because with its hooves it had dug two deep brown semicircles out of the grass. But we ate it all the same.

After this beginning, several pairs of specialized hunter-knackers were formed, who were no longer satisfied with felling sick or stray horses, but chose the fattest ones, enticed them out of the herd and then killed them in the wood. They preferred to work in the first light of dawn; one covered the animal's eyes with a cloth, while the other dealt the (not always) mortal blow on its neck.

It was a period of absurd abundance; there was horsemeat for everybody, without stint, gratis; the maximum the hunters would ask for a dead horse was two or three rations of tobacco. In every corner of the wood, and when it was raining even in the corridors and under the staircases in the Red House, men and women were to be seen busily cooking enormous horse steaks with mushrooms; it was thanks to these that we survivors of Auschwitz did not need many more months to regain our strength.

The Russians of the Command did not pay the slightest attention even to this plundering. Only once did they intervene, and only once did they inflict a punishment: towards the end of the migration, when horsemeat was already growing scarce and the price was beginning to rise, one of the ex-jailbirds had the impudence to open a real slaughterhouse, in one of the many garrets of the Red House. The Russians frowned on this enterprise, though it was not clear whether on hygienic or moral grounds; the culprit was publicly censured, declared a '*chort* (devil), *parazìt*, *spyekulànt*', and shut up in a cell.

It was not a very severe punishment: in the cell, for obscure reasons – perhaps through a bureaucratic atavism which looked back to a time when prisoners must long have been three to a cell – one was given three rations of food a day. It made no difference whether the prisoners were nine, or one, or none; the rations were always three. So the illegal butcher left his cell at the end of his punishment, after ten days of overeating, as fat as a pig and full of *joie de vivre*.

13. Holidays

As ALWAYS HAPPENS, the end of our hunger laid bare and perceptible in us a much deeper hunger. Not only desire for our homes, which in a sense was discounted and projected into the future; but a more immediate and urgent need for human contacts, for mental and physical work, for novelty and variety.

Life at Starye Dorogi, which would have been little less than perfect if it had been felt to be a holiday interlude in a workaday existence, began to weigh on us because of the very idleness it forced upon us. In these conditions, several people left to seek life and adventures elsewhere. It would be inaccurate to speak of a flight, because the camp was not fenced or guarded, and the Russians did not count us, or did not count us carefully; quite simply, they said good-bye to their friends and took off. They got what they were searching for: they saw countries and peoples, they went far afield, some as far as Odessa or Moscow, others as far as the frontiers; they experienced the lock-ups of isolated villages, the biblical hospitality of the peasants, vague love-affairs, stupid interrogations by duty-bound police, more hunger and solitude. Almost all returned to Starye Dorogi, because, even if there was not a trace of barbed wire around the Red House, when they tried to force the legendary frontier towards the West they found it severely barred.

They returned, and resigned themselves to our régime of limbo. The days of the Nordic summer were very long; it was already light at three in the morning, and the dusk dragged on tirelessly until nine or ten in the evening. The excursions into the woods, meals, sleep, risky bathes in the marshes, ever-repeated conversations, plans for the future, were not enough to shorten the time of our expectation, or to lighten its weight, which increased day by day.

We tried to approach the Russians, but with little success. The more sophisticated ones (who spoke German or English) acted in a courteous but diffident manner towards us, and often brusquely interrupted a conversation, as if they felt guilty or spied on. With the most simple-minded ones, the seventeen-year-old soldiers of the Command and the peasants of the neighbourhood, the difficulties of language reduced us to stunted and primordial relationships.

It is six in the morning, but the light of day has long since banished sleep. I am walking towards a thicket where there is a stream, with a pot of potatoes organized by Cesare; it is our favourite place for cooking operations because there is water and wood, and today it is my turn to wash the plates and cook. I light a fire between three stones; and to my surprise, I see a Russian not far away, small but sturdy, with thick Asiatic features, intent on preparations similar to mine. He has no matches; he approaches me, and as far as I can judge is asking me for a light. He is stripped to the waist, wearing only his army trousers, and his air is not very reassuring. He wears a bayonet at his waist.

I offer him a lighted stick; the Russian takes it, but stands there looking at me with suspicious curiosity. Is he thinking that my potatoes are stolen? Or is he meditating whether to take them away from me? Or has he mistaken me for someone he does not like?

No, something else is worrying him. He has realized that I do not speak Russian, and this vexes him. The fact that a man, adult and normal, cannot speak Russian, which means he cannot speak, seems to him to smack of insolent arrogance, as if I had flatly refused to reply to him. He is not ill-intentioned, in fact, he is prepared to give me a hand, to raise me from my guilty condition of ignorance; Russian is so easy, everybody speaks it, even children who have not yet started to walk. He sits beside me; I continue to be anxious for my potatoes, and watch him carefully; but, to judge by his appearance, he has nothing else on his mind except a desire to help me recover lost time. He does not understand, he does not admit my attitude of refusal; he wants to teach me his tongue.

Alas, as a teacher he is not worth much; he lacks method and patience, and, even worse, works on the mistaken assumption that I can follow his explanations and comments. So long as it is simply a question of terms, everything goes quite well, and in fact I quite enjoy the game. He points to a potato, and says: '*Kartòfel*'; then he grips my shoulder with his mighty paw, pushes his index finger in my face, listens intently like a deaf man, and waits. I repeat: '*Kartòfel*'. He puts on a disgusted expression; my pronunciation is wrong: I do not even know how to pronounce! He tries two or three times more, then he gets bored and tries a new word. '*Ogòn*', he says, pointing to the fire; that is better, apparently my repetition satisfies him. He looks around searching for other pedagogic objects, then stares at me with intensity, slowly rising to his feet as he does so, as if he wished to hypnotize me; then, in a flash, he whips his bayonet out of its scabbard and flourishes it in the air.

I jump to my feet and make off, towards the Red House: too bad about the potatoes. But after a few steps I hear an ogrish laugh echoing behind my back: his joke has been successful.

'*Britva*', he says to me, making the blade flash in the sun; and I repeat the word, feeling somewhat uneasy. With a slash worthy of a paladin, he slices a branch clean off a tree; he shows it to me, and says: '*Dèrevo*'. I repeat: '*Dèrevo*'.

'*Ya russky soldàt.*' I repeat, as best I can: '*Ya russky soldàt.*' Another laugh, which seems to me contemptuous: *he* is a Russian soldier, I am not, and that makes quite a difference. He explains this to me in a confused manner, with a torrent of words, pointing first at my chest, and then at his, and nodding yes and no with his head. Clearly he regards me as a worthless pupil, a desperate case of obtuseness; to my relief, he returns to his fire and abandons me to my barbarism.

On another day, but at the same time and in the same place, I come across an unaccustomed spectacle. A group of Italians surround a boyish Russian sailor, tall, with rapid agile movements. He is 'narrating' an episode of war; and because he knows that his language is not understood, he expresses himself as best he can, in a manner which for him is nearly as spontaneous as, if not more so than, words: he expresses himself with all his muscles, with the precocious furrows on his face, with flashing eyes and teeth, with leaps and gestures; and from this is born a *pas seul*, full of fascination and force.

It is night, '*noch*': palms down, he moves his hands slowly around him. Everything is silent: he pronounces a long 'ssh' with his index finger parallel to his nose. He narrows his eyes and points to the horizon: there, far away, are the Germans, '*niemtzy*'. How many? Five, he indicates with his fingers; '*finef*', he adds in Yiddish for greater clarity. With his hand he digs a small round hole in the sand, and lays five twigs flat in it, these are the Germans; then a sixth twig pointing sideways, the '*mashina*', the machine-gun. What are the Germans doing? Here his eyes light up with savage mirth: '*spats*', they are sleeping (and for a moment he himself snores); they are sleeping, the fools, and they do not know what is coming to them.

What did he do? This is what he did: he approached, cautiously, against the wind, like a leopard. Then, with a leap, he jumped into the nest pulling out his knife; and now he repeats his former actions, wholly lost in a dramatic ecstasy. The ambush, and the sudden atrocious scuffle, are repeated before our eyes; the man, his face transfigured by a tense sinister grin, turns into a whirlwind; he jumps forwards and backwards, striking in front of him, to his side, high up and low down, in an explosion of deadly energy; but it is a lucid fury, his weapon (which exists, a long knife which he has taken out of his boot) penetrates, slashes, rips open with ferocity, but at the same time with tremendous skill, a foot away from our faces.

Suddenly the sailor stops, slowly rises; his knife drops from his hand; he is panting, his eyes grow vacuous. He looks at the ground, as if amazed not to see the corpses and blood there; he looks around bewildered, emptied; he becomes aware of us, and gives us a childish timid smile. '*Koniechno*', he says: it is over; he walks slowly away.

Quite different, and just as mysterious then as it seems now, was the case of the Lieutenant. The Lieutenant (we were never able to learn his name, perhaps not by chance) was a young lean sallow Russian, perpetually frowning. He spoke Italian perfectly, with so slight a Russian accent that it could be mistaken for some Italian dialectal cadence; but, in contrast to all the other Russians of the Command, he showed little cordiality or sympathy towards us. He was the only person we were able to question. How was it he spoke Italian? Why was he with us? Why did they keep us in Russia four months after the end of the war? Were we hostages? Had we been forgotten? Why could we not write to Italy? When would we return? . . . But the Lieutenant replied to all these questions, which weighed as heavy as lead, in a curt, elusive manner, showing a self-confidence and authority which ill accorded with his not very elevated rank. We noticed that even his superiors treated him with a strange deference, as if they were afraid of him.

He kept the same surly aloofness from the Russians as from us. He never smiled, he did not drink, he would not accept invitations, or cigarettes; he spoke little, with cautious words which he seemed to weigh one by one. At his first appearances, we had naturally thought of him as our interpreter and delegate at the Russian Command, but we soon saw that his duties (if he had any, and if his behaviour was not merely a complicated manner of boosting his own importance) must have been different, and we preferred to stay silent in his presence. From a few reticent remarks of his we realized that he had a good knowledge of the topography of Turin and Milan. Had he been to Italy? 'No,' he replied curtly, and gave no other explanations.

Public health was excellent, and the patients at the surgery were few and always the same, with boils, the usual imaginary illnesses, a little scabies, a touch of colitis. One day a woman came, complaining of vague disturbances: nausea, backache, giddiness, attacks of sweating. Leonardo examined her; she had bruises almost everywhere, but told us not to pay attention to them, she had fallen down the stairs. A detailed diagnosis was not very easy with so few instruments available, but, by a process of elimination and by deduction from the numerous precedents among our women, Leonardo declared to his patient that she was probably in her third month of pregnancy. The woman showed no joy, anguish, surprise or indignation; she accepted the diagnosis, thanked him, but did not go away. She went back to sit on the bench in the corridor, silent and tranquil, as if she were waiting for someone.

She was a small, dark-haired girl, about twenty-five years old, with a homely air, submissive and absent; her face, which was not very attractive, nor very expressive, did not seem new to me, nor did her way of speaking, with gentle Tuscan inflections.

I had certainly met her somewhere, but not at Starye Dorogi. I felt an evanescent sensation of an overlap, of a transposition, of a marked inversion of relationships, which however I was unable to define. In a vague but insistent manner, I linked this feminine image to a knot of intense feelings: of a humble and distant admiration, of gratitude, frustration, fear, even of abstract desire, but above all of a deep and indeterminate anguish.

As she continued to sit on the bench, quiet and still, with no signs of impatience, I asked her if she wanted something, if she still had need of us; surgery was over, there were no other patients, it was time to close. 'No, no,' she replied; 'I don't need anything. I shall go now.'

Flora! The nebulous memory abruptly took shape, coagulated into a precise, definite picture, rich in retrospective details of time and place, colours, states of mind, atmosphere, smells. She was Flora: the Italian from the Buna cellars, the woman from the Lager, the object of Alberto's and my dreams for over a month, unwitting symbol of a lost and by then unhoped-for liberty. Flora, last seen only a year ago, and it seemed a century.

Flora was a small-time prostitute, who had ended in Germany with the Todt Organization. She did not know German and had learnt no trade, so she had been set to sweep the floors of the Buna factory. She swept all day, wearily, exchanging not a word with anyone, never raising her eyes from her broom and her endless work. Nobody seemed to bother about her, while for her part she hardly climbed to the upper floors, almost as if she feared the light of day; she swept the cellars interminably, from top to bottom, and then began again, like a sleepwalker.

She was the only woman we had seen for months, and she spoke our language, but we Häftlinge were forbidden to talk to her. To Alberto and myself she seemed beautiful, mysterious, incorporeal. Despite the prohibition, which in a sense multiplied the enchantment of our meetings by adding to them the pungent flavour of the illicit, we exchanged a few furtive phrases with Flora; we declared ourselves Italians, and asked her for bread. We asked her this reluctantly, only too aware that we were demeaning ourselves and the quality of this delicate human contact; but hunger, which rarely compromises, obliged us not to waste the occasion.

Flora often brought us bread, and gave it to us with a bewildered air, in the dark corners of the basement, sniffing back her tears. She was sorry for us, and would have liked to help us in other ways as well, but did not know how to and was afraid. Afraid of everything, like a defenceless animal; perhaps even of us, not directly, but in so far as we formed part of that foreign and incomprehensible world which had torn her from her country, had forced a broom into her hand, and had relegated her beneath the earth, to sweep floors already swept a hundred times.

For our part, we were upset, grateful and full of shame. We suddenly became aware of our miserable appearance and suffered because of it. Alberto, who used to wander around all day with his eyes fixed to the ground like a bloodhound, and so found the most curious oddments, picked up a comb somewhere, and solemnly gave it to Flora, who still possessed her hair; after that we felt tied to her by a gentle unsullied tie, and we dreamt of her at night. Consequently we felt acute discomfort, an absurd and impotent mixture of jealousy and disillusionment, when we were forced by the evidence to realize, to admit to ourselves, that Flora had meetings with other men. Where and how and with whom? In the least attractive place and manner; not far away, in the hay, in a clandestine warren organized in a basement by a co-operative of German and Polish Kapos. Little was needed: a wink, an imperious nod of the head, and Flora laid down her broom and docilely followed the man of the moment. After a few minutes she returned alone; she adjusted her clothes and began to sweep again without looking us in the face. After this squalid discovery, Flora's bread was bitter to our taste, not that this stopped us from accepting and eating it.

I did not identify myself to Flora, through charity towards her and towards myself. Faced with these phantasms, of my Buna self, of the woman of my memories and of this reincarnation, I felt changed, intensely 'different', like a butterfly before a caterpillar. In the limbo of Starye Dorogi I felt dirty, ragged, tired, burdened, exhausted by expectation, yet young and full of vigour, looking towards the future; but Flora had not changed. Now she lived with a cobbler from Bergamo, not as a wife, but as a slave. She washed and cooked for him, and followed him with humble subdued eyes; the man, bulllike and apish, watched every step of hers, and beat her savagely at every trace of suspicion. Hence the bruises all over her; she had come to the surgery stealthily, and was now afraid to go out to meet her master's anger.

At Starye Dorogi no-one demanded anything of us, no-one importuned us, no pressure was placed on us, we did not have to defend ourselves from anything; we felt as inert and settled as an alluvial sediment. In this sluggish uneventful life of ours, the arrival of a Soviet military film truck marked a memorable date. It must have been a travelling unit, formerly in service with the troops at the front or in the supply lines, and now itself on its way home; it included a projector, a generating plant, a supply of films and the personnel to run it. It stopped at Starye Dorogi for three days, and gave a performance each evening.

The shows took place in the theatre hall; it was very spacious, and the seats carried off by the Germans had been replaced by rustic benches of unstable equilibrium on the floor which rose from the screen towards the gallery. The gallery, which also sloped, had been reduced to a narrow strip; the highest part had been divided in a moment of caprice by the mysterious and whimsical architects of the Red House into a series of small rooms without air or light, whose doors opened towards the stage. The unattached women of our colony lived there.

On the first evening an old Austrian film was shown, in itself mediocre, and of little interest to the Russians, but full of emotional charge for us Italians. It was a silent film about war and spying, with sub-titles in German: more exactly, it was about an episode of the First World War on the Italian front. The same candour and rhetorical equipment appeared as in analogous films of Allied production: military honour, sacred frontiers, soldiers of great heroism who nevertheless burst into tears as easily as virgins, bayonet attacks carried out with improbable enthusiasm. Only it was all turned upside down: the Austro-Hungarians, officers and soldiers, were noble and sturdy characters, valiant and chivalrous, with the spiritual sensitive faces of stoic warriors, the rough and honest faces of peasants, inspiring sympathy at the first glance. The Italians, all of them, were a crowd of vulgar numbskulls, all marked by striking and laughable physical defects: they were cross-eyed, obese, with narrow shoulders, bandy legs and low sloping foreheads. They were cowardly and ferocious, brutal and dimwitted; the officers had faces like effete dandies, crushed under the incongruous weight of kettle-like hats familiar to us from portraits of the generals Cadorna and Diaz; the soldiers had porcine or apish faces, accentuated by the helmets of our fathers, worn aslant or pulled down over their eyes treacherously to hide their looks.

The arch-villain, an Italian spy at Vienna, was a strange chimera, half D'Annunzio and half Victor Emmanuel, of such absurdly small stature that he was forced to look up at everybody; he wore a monocle and a bow-tie, and paced up and down the screen with arrogant strides like a cockerel. When he returned to the Italian lines, he coldly superintended the shooting of ten innocent Tyrolean civilians.

We Italians, so little accustomed to seeing ourselves cast as the 'enemy', odious by definition, and so dismayed at being hated by anybody, derived a complex pleasure from watching the film – a pleasure not without disquiet, a source of salutary meditations.

On the second evening a Soviet film was announced, and the audience began to warm up; the Italians, because it was the first one they saw; the Russians, because the title promised a war film, full of movement and shooting. The word got round; Russian soldiers arrived unexpectedly from nearby and distant garrisons, and thronged outside the doors of the theatre. When the doors opened, they burst inside like a river in flood, climbing noisily over the benches and jostling against each other with much pushing and shoving.

The film was ingenuous and uncomplicated. A Soviet military plane was forced to land in an unspecified mountainous area near the frontier; it was a small two-seater plane, with only the pilot on board. Just as he had repaired the engine and was about to take off, a local notable advanced, a turbaned sheikh with an extraordinarily suspicious air, who, with flattering bows and oriental obeisances, begged to be taken on board. Even an idiot would have understood that he was a dangerous rogue, probably a smuggler, a dissident leader or a foreign agent; but as it was, the pilot, with thoughtless generosity, gave way to his prolix entreaties, and placed him in the back seat of the plane.

We were shown the take-off, and some magnificent panoramic views of mountain ranges sparkling with glaciers (I think it was the Caucasus); then the sheikh, with secret viperous movements, took a revolver from under his cloak, pushed it in the pilot's back and ordered him to change course. The pilot, who did not even turn round, reacted with lightning decision; he reared the plane into a sharp loop. The sheikh collapsed in his seat, overwhelmed by fear and nausea; but instead of putting him out of action, the pilot tranquilly continued the flight towards his destination. After a few minutes, and more admirable mountain scenery, the bandit recovered; he dragged himself towards the pilot, once more raised his revolver and repeated the attempt. This time the plane went into a nose dive, and plunged down for some thousands of feet, towards an inferno of precipitous peaks and abysses; the sheikh fainted and the plane regained height. So the flight continued for more than an hour, with continually repeated aggressions by the Muslim, and ever new acrobatics by the pilot; until after a final attempt by the sheikh, who seemed to have nine lives like a cat, the plane went into a spin; clouds, mountains and glaciers whirled boldly round it, until finally it came down safely on its predetermined landing-field. The inanimate sheikh was handcuffed; the pilot, as fresh as a rose, was not subjected to an inquiry, but had his hand shaken by proud superiors, was promoted on the field, and received a shy kiss from a girl who seemed to have been waiting for him for some time.

The Russian soldiers in the audience followed the clumsy plot with noisy passion, applauding the hero and insulting the traitor; but it was nothing compared to what happened on the third evening.

Hurricane was announced for the third evening, quite a good American film of the 'thirties. A Polynesian sailor, a modern version of the 'noble savage', a simple man, strong and mild, is vulgarly provoked in a bar by a group of drunken whites, and wounds one of them slightly. Reason is clearly on his side, but no-one testifies in his favour; he is arrested, tried, and, to his pathetic incomprehension, condemned to a month in prison. He holds out only for a few days; not only because of an almost animal-like need of liberty and intolerance of bondage, but above all because he feels, he knows, that not he but the whites have violated justice; if this is the law of the whites, then the law is unjust. He knocks down a guard and escapes amid a shower of bullets.

Now the mild sailor has become a real criminal. He is hunted all over the archipelago, but it is pointless searching so far; he has returned quietly to his village. He is taken again, and relegated to a distant island, condemned to hard labour, and endures toil and beatings. He escapes again, throws himself into the sea from a vertiginous cliff, steals a canoe and sails for days towards his homeland, without food or water; he reaches it exhausted, just as the hurricane promised by the title is threatening to break. The hurricane bursts out at once wildly, and the man, like a good American hero, fights alone against the elements, and saves not only his woman, but the church, the pastor, and all the faithful who had thought they would find shelter in the church. Rehabilitated, with his girl at his side, he advances towards a happy future, under the sun which breaks through the disappearing clouds.

This story, typically individualistic, elementary and not badly told, aroused the Russians to seismic enthusiasm. An hour before the beginning, a tumultuous crowd (attracted by the poster, which portrayed a magnificent Polynesian girl, scantily dressed) was already pushing against the doors; they were almost all very young soldiers, armed. It was clear that there was not room for everybody in the large theatre, not even standing; for this very reason they fought doggedly with their elbows to gain entrance. One fell, was trampled on, and came the next day to the surgery; we thought we should find him smashed up, but he only had a few bruises: a people of solid bones. Soon the doors were broken open, smashed to pieces and the pieces used as clubs; when the film started, the crowd which stood crushed inside the theatre was already highly excited and bellicose.

It seemed as if the people in the film were not shadows to them, but flesh and blood friends or enemies, near at hand. The sailor was acclaimed at every exploit, greeted by noisy cheers and sten-guns brandished perilously over their heads. The policemen and jailers were insulted with bloodthirsty cries, greeted with shouts of 'leave him alone', 'go away', 'I'll get you', 'kill them all'. After the first escape, when the exhausted and wounded fugitive was once more captured, and even worse, sneered at and derided by the sardonic asymmetrical mask of John Carradine, pandemonium broke out. The audience stood up shouting, in generous defence of the innocent man; a wave of avengers moved threateningly towards the screen, but were cursed at and checked in turn by less heated elements or by those who wanted to see the end. Stones, lumps of earth, splinters from the demolished doors, even a regulation boot flew against the screen, hurled with furious precision at the odious face of the great enemy, which shone forth oversize in the foreground.

When the long and vigorous scene of the hurricane was reached, a witches' sabbath ensued. One could hear the sharp cries of the few women who had remained trapped in the crowd; a pole appeared, then another one, passed from hand to hand above our heads, amid deafening shouts. At first we could not understand what they were meant for, then the design became clear; it had probably been planned by the excluded Russians, who were creating an uproar outside. They were attempting an escalade of the gynaeceum-gallery.

The poles were raised and rested against the balcony, and various enthusiasts took off their boots and began to clamber up, as they do with greasy poles at a village fair. From this moment the spectacle of the escalade distracted all attention from the other spectacle which continued on the screen. As soon as one of the aspirants managed to climb above the tide of heads, he was pulled down by his feet and dragged back to the ground by ten or twenty hands. Groups of supporters and adversaries formed; one bold man managed to free himself from the crowd and pull himself up by his arms, followed by another one on the same pole. When they had almost reached the height of the balcony they fought among themselves for a few minutes, the lower one grabbing the other one's heels, the latter defending himself by kicking out blindly. At the same time, on the balcony, one could see the heads of a group of Italians, who had hastily climbed up the tortuous stairs of the Red House to protect the besieged women; the pole, pushed back by the defenders, oscillated, balanced for a long moment in a vertical position, then crashed among the crowd like a pine tree cut down by woodsmen, with the two men clinging to it. At this point, whether by chance or through a wise intervention of the authorities, the projector lamp went out, everything plunged into darkness, the noise of the pit reached a fearful intensity and everybody poured out into the moonlit night amid shouts, oaths and acclamations.

To everyone's regret, the cinema troupe left the next morning. The following evening a renewed and bold Russian attempt to invade the feminine quarters occurred, this time across the roofs and gutters; after this, a night patrol of Italian volunteers was set up. Furthermore, the women in the gallery decamped as an extra precaution, and joined the larger part of the feminine population, in a collective dormitory; a less intimate but securer arrangement.

14. The Theatre

ABOUT THE MIDDLE of August a meeting ground with the
Russians was found. Despite professional secrecy, the whole
camp soon knew that the 'Rumanians' were organizing a
revue, with the agreement and approval of the authorities;
auditions took place in the theatre, whose doors had been
restored as well as possible, and which was guarded by pickets
who refused entry to all outsiders. Among the acts in the
revue, there was a tap-dance: the specialist, an extremely
conscientious sailor, practised every evening, among a small
circle of experts and consultants. Now, tap-dancing is noisy
by its very nature; the Lieutenant passed nearby, heard the
rhythmic noise, forced the picket, in which he was clearly
exceeding his authority, and entered. He watched two or
three sessions, to the discomfort of the bystanders, without
emerging from his habitual reserve and without relaxing his
hermetic mask; then, unexpectedly, he informed the organizing committee that he was a passionate fan of tap-dancing
in his spare time, and that he had long wanted to learn
exactly how to tap-dance; so the dancer was invited, indeed
ordered, to give him a series of lessons.

The spectacle of these lessons so interested me that I
found a way of watching, slipping through the back ways of
the Red House and hiding myself in a dark corner. The
Lieutenant was the best pupil imaginable: very serious,
willing, tenacious and physically gifted. He danced in his
uniform, with boots, for exactly one hour a day, without
allowing his teacher or himself a moment's rest. He made
very rapid progress.

When the revue opened, a week later, the tap-dance number was a surprise to everybody; teacher and pupil danced, faultlessly, with impeccable parallelism and synchronism; the teacher, winking and smiling, dressed in an extravagant gypsy costume created by the women; the Lieutenant, funereal, with his nose in the air and his eyes fixed on the ground, as if he was performing a sacrificial dance. Naturally, he was in uniform, with his medals on his chest and his holster on his belt dancing with him.

They were applauded; equally applauded were several other not very original numbers (a few Neapolitan songs from the classical repertory: *I Pompieri di Viggiu**, a sketch in which a lover conquers his girl's heart with a bunch not of flowers, but of *ribba*, our stinking daily fish; the *Montanara** sung in chorus, with Mr Unverdorben leading the choir). But two rather unusual numbers gained an enthusiastic, and well-merited, success.

A large fat person came on the stage, with hesitant steps, and legs wide apart, masked, muffled and bundled up, like the famous Michelin man. He greeted the public like an athlete, with his hands clasped above his head; meantime, two assistants, with great effort, rolled alongside him an enormous piece of equipment consisting of a bar and two wheels, like those used by weight-lifters.

He bent down, gripped the bar, tensed all his muscles; nothing happened, the bar did not move. Then he took off his cloak, folded it meticulously, placed it on the ground and prepared for another attempt. When the weight again did not move from the ground, he took off a second cloak, placing it next to the first; and so on with various cloaks, civilian and military cloaks, raincoats, cassocks, greatcoats. The athlete diminished in volume visibly, the stage filled up with garments and the weight seemed to have grown roots in the ground.

* Popular songs, originating in the Second World War.

When he had finished with the cloaks, he began to take off jackets of all kinds (among them a Häftling striped jacket, in honour of our minority), then shirts in abundance, always trying to lift the instrument with punctilious solemnity after each piece of clothing had been removed, and renouncing the attempt without the least sign of impatience or surprise. However, when he took off his fourth or fifth shirt, he suddenly stopped. He looked at the shirt with attention, first at arm's length, then close up; he searched the collar and seams with agile monkey-like movements, and then with his thumb and forefinger pulled out an imaginary louse. He examined it, his eyes dilated with horror, placed it delicately on the ground, drew a circle around it with chalk, turned back, with a single hand snatched the bar from the ground, which for the occasion had become as light as a feather, and crushed the louse with one clean blow.

After this rapid parenthesis, he continued taking off shirts, trousers, socks and body-belts with gravity and composure, trying in vain to lift the weight. In the end, he stood in his pants, in the middle of a mountain of clothing; he took off his mask, and the public recognized in him the sympathetic and popular cook Gridacucco, small, dry, hopping and bustling, aptly nicknamed 'Scannagrillo' (Cricket Butcher) by Cesare. Applause burst out: Scannagrillo looked around bewildered, then, as if seized by sudden stage-fright, picked up his weight, which was probably made of cardboard, put it under his arm and scampered off.

The other great success was the 'Three-Cornered Hat' song. It is a song totally lacking in sense, which consists of a single, continually repeated quatrain ('My hat has got three corners – three corners has my hat – if it did not have three corners – it would not be my hat'), and is sung to a tune so trite and custom-worn that its origin is now unknown. However, its characteristic is that, at every repeat, one of the words of the quatrain is omitted, and replaced by a gesture:

a concave hand on the head for 'hat', a fist touching the chest for 'my', fingers drawn together as they rise, to represent the surface of a cone, for 'corners'; and so on, until, with the final elimination, the strophe is reduced to a stunted stuttering of articles and conjunctions which cannot be expressed by signs, or, according to another version, by total silence scanned by rhythmic gestures.

In the heterogeneous group of the 'Rumanians' there must have been someone who had the theatre in his blood; in their interpretation, this infantile whimsicality turned into a sinister, obscurely allegorical pantomime, full of symbolic and disquieting echoes.

A small orchestra, whose instruments had been provided by the Russians, began the tired motif, in low muted tones. Slowly swaying to the rhythm, three nightmare figures came on to the stage; they were wrapped up in black cloaks, with black hoods on their heads, and from the hoods emerged three faces, of corpse-like, decrepit pallor, marked by deep livid lines. They entered with a hesitant dance step, holding three long unlighted candles in their hands. When they reached the centre of the stage, always in time to the rhythm, they bowed towards the public with senile difficulty, slowly bending their stiff joints, with small worrying wrenches; they took two full minutes to bend down and rise again, minutes which were full of anguish for all the spectators. They painfully regained an erect position, the orchestra stopped, and the three phantoms began to sing the stupid strophe in a tremulous broken voice. They sang; and at every repeat, with the accumulation of gaps replaced by uncertain gestures, it seemed as if life, as well as voice, would drain from them. With the rhythm accentuated by the hypnotic pulsation of a single muted drum, the paralysis proceeded slowly and ineluctably. The final repetition, with absolute silence from orchestra, singers and public, was an excruciating agony, a death throe.

When the song ended, the orchestra began again lugubri-ously; the three figures, with a final effort, trembling in every limb, repeated their bow. Unbelievably they once more managed to straighten themselves, and with their candles wavering, with a horrible and macabre hesitation, but always in time to the rhythm, they disappeared for ever behind the scenes.

The 'Three-Cornered Hat' number took away one's breath, and every evening was greeted with a silence more eloquent than applause. Why? Perhaps because, under the grotesque appearance, one perceived the heavy breath of a collective dream, of the dream emanating from exile and idleness, when work and troubles have ceased, and nothing acts as a screen between a man and himself; perhaps because we saw the impotence and nullity of our life and of life itself, and the hunch-backed crooked profiles of the monsters generated by the sleep of reason.

More innocuous, indeed puerile and burlesque, was the allegory of the next programme to be arranged. It was already obvious from the title, *The Shipwreck of the Spiritless*; we were the spiritless, we Italians lost on our way home, grown used to an existence of inertia and boredom; the desert island was Starye Dorogi; and the cannibals were ostenta-tiously the worthy Russians of the Command. One hundred per cent cannibals; they appeared on the stage naked and tattooed, prattled in some primitive and unintelligible jargon, fed on raw and bloody human meat. Their leader lived in a hut made of branches, he had a white slave permanently on all fours as a seat, and on his chest hung a large alarm clock which he consulted, not to tell the time, but to read the omens for governmental decisions. Comrade Colonel, in charge of our camp, must have been a man of wit, or ex-tremely forbearing, or else just dim, to have authorized so harsh a caricature of his person and office; or perhaps, once more, it was a question of the age-old beneficent

184

Russian insouciance, of that Oblomovian negligence, which was to be found at all levels at that happy moment of their history.

In truth, once at least the suspicion crossed our minds that the Command had not digested the satire, or that it regretted its decision. After the first performance of *The Shipwreck*, all hell broke loose in the Red House in the middle of the night; yells in the dormitories, kicks at the doors, commands in Russian, Italian and bad German. Those of us who had come from Katowice, and had already witnessed a similar upheaval, were only half frightened; the others lost their heads (the 'Rumanians' in particular, who were responsible for the script); rumour of a Russian reprisal immediately went round, and the most apprehensive were already thinking of Siberia.

The Lieutenant acted as intermediary, and on this occasion seemed even more gloomy and sullen than usual; through him, the Russians made us all get up and dress hastily, and line up in one of the winding passages of the building. Half an hour, an hour passed, and nothing happened; at the end of the queue, where I was in one of the last places, nobody knew where the head began, nor did the line move forward a step. Beside the possibility of a reprisal for the *Spiritless*, the rashest of hypotheses ran through the line: the Russians had decided to search out the Fascists; they were looking for the two girls in the wood; they were subjecting us to an examination for V.D.; they were recruiting people to work in the *kolkhoz*; they were looking for specialists, like the Germans. Then we saw an Italian pass by beaming cheerfully. He said: 'They're giving out money!' and shook a wad of rubles in his hand. No-one believed him; but a second, then a third one passed and they all confirmed the information. The incident was never clearly understood (but then, who ever fully understood why we were at Starye Dorogi, and what we were doing there?); according to the most sensible interpretation, it seems probable that we had been equated with prisoners of war, at least by some Soviet departments, and so were owed compensation for the days of work we had carried out. But what criterion was used to compute these days (hardly any of us had ever worked for the Russians, either at Starye Dorogi or before); why they also paid the children, and above all, why the ceremony had to occur so tumultuously between two and six in the morning – all this is destined to remain obscure.

The Russians distributed salaries varying from thirty to eighty rubles a head, either following inscrutable criteria, or haphazardly. They were not huge sums, but they pleased everyone; they were equivalent to luxuries for a few days. At dawn we returned to bed, commenting on the event in different ways; no-one understood that it was a good omen, a prelude to repatriation.

But from that day, even without an official announcement, the signs multiplied. Tenuous, uncertain, timid signs; but enough to spread the sensation that something was finally moving, something was about to happen. A patrol of young Russian soldiers arrived, baby-faced and lost; they told us that they had come from Austria, and would soon have to leave again to escort a convoy of foreigners; but they did not know where. The Command, after months of useless petitions, distributed shoes to all in need of them. Finally, the Lieutenant disappeared, as if he had been assumed into Heaven.

It was all extremely vague, and not a little ambiguous. Even granting that a departure was imminent, what assurance was there that it was a repatriation, and not another transfer to heaven knows where? The long experience we had by now acquired of Russian methods counselled us to temper our hopes with a salutary coefficient of doubt. The season also contributed to our disquiet; in the first weeks of September the sun and sky clouded over, the air became cold and damp, and the first rain fell to remind us of the precariousness of our situation.

The road, meadows and fields changed into a desolate marsh. Water leaked through the roofs of the Red House in abundance, dripping pitilessly on the bunks at night; yet more water entered through the glassless windows. None of us had heavy clothes. In the village we saw peasants coming back from the wood with carts of faggots and branches; others were patching up their houses, adjusting the thatched roofs; all of them, even the women, wore boots. The wind carried a new alarming smell from their homes; the bitter smoke of damp wood burning, the smell of approaching winter. Another winter, the third one – and what a winter!

But finally the announcement came: the announcement of our return, of our salvation, of the conclusion of our lengthy wanderings. It came in two novel unusual ways, from two different sides, and was convincing and open and dissipated all anxiety. It came in the theatre and through the theatre, and it came along the muddy road, carried by a strange and illustrious messenger.

It was night, it was raining, and in the crowded theatre (what else could one do in the evening, before slipping between the damp sheets?) there was a repeat performance of *The Shipwreck of the Spiritless*, perhaps the ninth or tenth. This *Shipwreck* made a shapeless but savoury dish, enlivened by its sharp and good-natured allusions to our everyday life; we had all followed it, every line of it, and by now we knew it by heart, and at every performance we were less inclined to laugh at the scene in which a Cantarella even more savage than the original built a huge metal pot to order for the Russian-cannibals, who intended to cook the leading Dispirited bigwigs in it; and every time the final scene, when the ship arrived, cut deeper.

Because there was, and clearly had to be, a scene in which a sail appeared on the horizon, and all the castaways ran laughing and crying on to the inhospitable beach. Now, just as the doyen among them, white haired and by now bowed from the interminable wait, pointed his finger towards the sea and shouted: 'A sail!' and just as all of us, with a lump in our throats, got ready for the traditional happy ending of the final scene, and for our retirement once more to our bunks, we heard a sudden thud, and saw the cannibal chief, a veritable *Deus ex machina*, fall vertically on to the stage, as if from the sky. He tore the alarm clock from his neck, the ring from his nose and the band of feathers from his head, and shouted in a thunderous voice: 'Tomorrow we leave!'

We were taken by surprise, and at first did not understand. Perhaps it was a joke? But the savage pursued: 'I am telling the truth, this is not theatre, this time it's real! The telegram has arrived, tomorrow we are all going home!' This time it was we Italians, spectators, actors and stagehands, who immediately overwhelmed the terrified Russians, who had understood nothing of this scene, which was not in the script. We emerged from the hall in disorder, and at first there was an anxious exchange of questions without answers; but then we saw the Colonel, surrounded by Italians, nodding assent, and we understood that the hour had come. We lit fires in the woods, and no-one slept; we spent the rest of the night singing and dancing, recalling past adventures, and remembering our lost companions – for it is not given to man to enjoy uncontaminated happiness.

The next morning, while the Red House was already buzzing and humming like a beehive whose swarm is about to leave, we saw a small car approach along the road. Very few passed by, so our curiosity was aroused, especially as it was not a military car. It slowed down in front of the camp, turned and entered, bouncing on the rough surface in front of the bizarre façade. Then we saw that it was a car all of us knew well, a Fiat 500A, a *Topolino*, rusty and decrepit, with the suspension piteously deformed.

It stopped in front of the entrance, and was at once surrounded by a crowd of inquisitive people. An extraordinary figure emerged, with great effort. It went on and on emerging; it was a very tall, corpulent, rubicund man, in a uniform we had never seen before: a Soviet General, a Generalissimo, a Marshal. When all of him had finally emerged from the door, the minute bodywork rose a good six inches, and the springs seemed to breathe more freely. The man was literally larger than the car, and it was incomprehensible how he had got inside. His conspicuous dimensions were further increased and accentuated, when he took a black object from the car, and unfolded it. It was a cloak, which hung down to the ground from two long wooden epaulettes; with an easy gesture, which gave evidence of his familiarity with the garment, he swung it over his back and fastened it to his shoulders, with the result that his outline, which had appeared plump, became angular. Seen from behind, the man was a monumental black rectangle one yard by two, who strode with majestic symmetry towards the Red House, amid two rows of perplexed people over whom he towered by a full head. How would he get through the door, as wide as he was? But he bent the two epaulettes backwards, like two wings, and entered.

This celestial messenger, who travelled alone through the mud in a cheap ancient ramshackle car, was Marshal Timoshenko in person, Semyòn Konstantinovich Timoshenko, the hero of the Bolshevik revolution, of Karelia and Stalingrad. After his reception by the local Russians, which was singularly sober and lasted only a few minutes, he emerged once more from the building and chatted unaffectedly with us Italians, like the rough Kutuzov in *War and Peace*, on the meadow, in the middle of the pots with fish on the boil, and the washing hung out to dry. He spoke Rumanian fluently with the 'Rumanians' (because he was, in fact is, a native of Bessarabia), and even knew a little Italian. The damp wind ruffled his grey hair, which contrasted with his ruddy sun-tanned complexion, that of a soldier, an eater and a drinker; he told us that it was really true; we were to leave soon, very soon; 'War over, everybody home'; the escort was ready, the supplies for the journey as well, the papers were in order. Within a few days the train would be waiting for us at Starye Dorogi station.

15. From Starye Dorogi to Iasi

NOBODY WAS REALLY surprised that the departure was not
to be expected 'tomorrow' in a literal sense, as the savage had
said in the theatre. On various occasions already we had been
able to verify that the corresponding Russian term, by one of
those semantic lapses which never occur without a reason,
had come to mean something far less definite and peremptory
than our 'tomorrow' and, in harmony with Russian habits,
meant rather 'one of the following days', 'sometime or other',
'in the near future'; in short, the rigorous temporal deter-
minant is softly blurred. We were not surprised, nor were we
particularly aggrieved. Once our departure was certain, we
became aware, to our own amazement, that this endless land,
these fields and woods which had witnessed the battle to
which we owed our salvation, these virgin primordial hori-
zons, this vigorous people full of the love of life, had entered
our hearts, had penetrated into us, and would remain there
for a long time, glorious and living images of a unique
season of our existence.

So not 'tomorrow', but a few days after the announcement,
on 15th September, 1945, we left the Red House in a troupe
and reached the station of Starye Dorogi in a festive mood.
The train was there, it was waiting for us, it was not an illusion of our senses; there was coal and water, and the engine,
enormous and majestic like a monument of itself, stood at the
right end. We hastened to touch its side: alas, it was cold.
There were sixty trucks, goods trucks, somewhat the worse
for wear, standing in a siding. We invaded them with jubilant
fury, and without quarrels; there were fourteen hundred of
us, or twenty to twenty-five persons to a truck, which, in

comparison with our many previous railway experiences, meant travelling comfortably and restfully.

The train did not leave at once, in fact, not until the following day; and it was clearly useless interrogating the head of the minute station, for he knew nothing. Only two or three trains passed during this time, and none stopped, none even slowed down. When one of them approached, the stationmaster waited for it on the platform, holding up a garland of branches with a sack hanging from it; the engine-driver leant out of the engine as it rushed by, with his right arm hooked. He seized the garland, and immediately threw a similar one to the ground, also with a sack; this was the postal service, Starye Dorogi's only contact with the rest of the world.

Apart from this, everything was immobile and quiet. Around the station, which was on a slight elevation, the prairies extended interminably, delimited only to the west by the black line of the woods and cut by the giddy ribbon of the railway line. Cattle grazed in herds, few and scattered at wide intervals; this was all there was to break the uniformity of the plain. During the long evening of our vigil, we could hear the songs of the shepherds, tenuous and modulated; one began, a second replied some miles away, then another and yet another, from every side of the horizon, until it seemed as if the very earth were singing.

We prepared for the night. After so many months and displacements, we now formed an organized community; consequently, we had not distributed ourselves casually in the trucks, but according to spontaneous nuclei of cohabitation. The 'Rumanians' occupied about ten trucks; three belonged to the San Vittore thieves, who did not want anybody and whom nobody wanted; another three were for the single women; four or five were taken by the couples, legitimate or otherwise; two, divided into two floors by a horizontal partition, and conspicuous because of the laundry hanging out to dry, belonged to families with children. The most striking of all was the orchestra-car: the entire theatrical company resided there, with all their instruments (including a piano), kindly donated by the Russians at the moment of departure. On Leonardo's initiative, our truck had been designated the hospital-car; a presumptuous and hopeful title as Leonardo possessed only a syringe and a stethoscope, while the wooden floor was as hard as that of the other trucks; however, there was not even one sick person in the whole train, nor did a single patient present himself during the entire journey. There were about twenty of us, among whom were, naturally, Cesare and Daniele, and, less naturally, the Moor, Mr Unverdorben, Giacomantonio and the Velletrano; besides these, there were about fifteen ex-P.O.W.s.

We spent the night drowsing restlessly on the bare floor of the truck. Day came; the engine was smoking, the driver was at his post, waiting with Olympian calm for the boiler to build up pressure. In the middle of the morning the engine roared, with a marvellous, deep metallic voice; it shook, vomited black smoke, the stay rods tightened, and the wheels began to turn. We looked at each other, almost bewildered. We had resisted, after all; we had won. After the year of Lager, of anguish and patience, after the wave of death that followed the liberation, after the cold and hunger, the contempt and haughty company of the Greek, after the illness and misery of Katowice, after the senseless journeys which had made us feel condemned to orbit for eternity in Russian space, like useless spent stars, after the idleness and bitter nostalgia of Starye Dorogi, we were rising once more, travelling upwards, on the journey home. Time, after two years of paralysis, had regained vigour and value, was once more working for us, and this put an end to the torpor of the long summer, to the threat of the approaching winter, and made us impatient, hungry for the days and miles ahead.

But soon, from the very first hours of the journey, we were

to realize that the hour of impatience had not yet sounded; the happy journey promised to be long and laborious and not without surprises; a small railroad Odyssey within our greater Odyssey. Patience was still needed, in unforeseeable doses; yet more patience.

Our train was over five hundred yards long; the trucks were in a poor condition, the track also, the velocity derisory, not more than twenty to thirty miles an hour. The railway line was single tracked; the stations with a siding sufficiently long to permit halts were few: the train often had to be uncoupled into two or three parts and pushed on to side lines with complicated and sluggish manoeuvres, so as to allow other trains to pass through.

There were no authorities on board, except for the engine-driver and the escort, which consisted of the seven eighteen-year-old soldiers who had come from Austria to pick us up. Although they were armed to the teeth, they were plain, well-mannered creatures, gentle and naïve, as cheerful and happy-go-lucky as schoolboys on holiday, and totally lacking in authority and practical sense. Every time the train stopped, we saw them walking up and down the platform, with their weapons slung from their shoulders and a proud officious air. They paraded their importance as though they were escorting a convoy of dangerous criminals, but it was all on the surface; we soon realized that their inspection concentrated increasingly on the two family trucks, half-way down the train. They were not attracted by the young wives, but by the vaguely domestic atmosphere which emanated from those itinerant gypsy-like dwellings, and which reminded them perhaps of their distant homes and their recent childhood; but above all they were allured by the children, so much so that, after the first halt, they chose the family trucks as their daily domicile, and returned to the truck reserved for them only at night. They were courteous and obliging; they willingly helped the mothers, went to get water and chop wood for the stoves. They struck up a curious and one-sided friendship with the Italian children. They learnt various games from them, including that of the circuit: this is a game played with marbles rolled along a complicated path. In Italy it is supposed to be related to the *Giro**; so the enthusiasm with which these young Russians assimilated it seemed strange to us, as there are few bicycles in Russia, and cycle races do not exist. At all events, for them it was a discovery: it was not unusual to see the seven Russians leave their sleeping-truck at the first stop in the morning, run to the family trucks, open the doors authoritatively, and pick up the still sleepy children and put them on the ground. Then they cheerfully dug out the circuit in the ground with their bayonets, and plunged into the game in great haste, on all fours with their weapons on their backs, anxious not to lose even a moment before the engine whistled.

On the evening of the 16th we reached Bobruisk, on the evening of the 17th Ovruch; and we realized that we were repeating the course of our last journey north, which had taken us from Zhmerinka to Slutsk and to Starye Dorogi, but in the opposite direction. We spent the interminable days partly sleeping, partly chatting or watching the majestic deserted steppe unfolding before our eyes. From the first days, our optimism lost a little of its shine; this journey of ours, which all appearances led us to hope would be the last, had been organized by the Russians in the vaguest and most careless of ways; or rather, it seemed as if it had not been organized at all, but decided by heaven knows whom, heaven knows where, with a simple stroke of the pen. In the whole train there were only two or three maps, disputed endlessly, on which we traced our problematic progress with difficulty; it was quite clear that we were travelling south, but with an exasperating slowness and irregularity, with

* Annual cycle race around the country.

incomprehensible deviations and stops, sometimes travelling only a few dozen miles in twenty-four hours. We often went to interrogate the engine-driver (there was no point in talking to the escort; they seemed happy merely to be travelling in a train, and it was of no importance to them to know where they were or where they were going); but the engine-driver, who emerged like a god of the underworld from his fiery cabin, spread out his arms, shrugged his shoulders, swept his hand in a semicircle from east to west, and replied every time: 'Where are we going tomorrow? I don't know, dear friends, I don't know. We are going where we find railway tracks.'

The person who endured the uncertainty and enforced idleness worst of all of us was Cesare. He sat in a corner of the truck, hypochondriacal and bristling, like a sick animal, and did not judge the countryside outside, or us inside the truck, worthy of a single glance. But his was a specious inertia; people in need of activity find opportunities everywhere. As we ran through a district covered with small villages, between Ovruch and Zhitomir, his attention was attracted by a brass ring worn by Giacomantonio, his shifty ex-partner from the Katowice market.

'Will you sell it to me?' he asked him.

'No,' Giacomantonio replied laconically, just as a start.

'I'll give you two rubles.'

'I want eight.'

The bargaining continued for a long time; it seemed clear that both found in it a diversion, an agreeable mental exercise, and that the ring was only a pretext, an excuse for a sort of friendly game, a practice bargain so as not to lose their skill. But it was not so; Cesare, as always, had conceived an exact plan.

To everybody's amazement, he yielded quickly, and acquired the ring, which he seemed to prize enormously, for four rubles, a figure grossly disproportionate to the value of the object. Then he withdrew into his corner, and dedicated the rest of the afternoon to mysterious exercises, driving away with angry snarls all inquisitive people who asked him questions (the most insistent was Giacomantonio). He had taken pieces of different quality cloth from his pockets, and diligently polished the ring, inside and out, breathing on it every now and again. Then he took out a packet of cigarette paper, and carefully continued his work with it, with extreme delicacy, no longer touching the metal with his fingers; occasionally, he would lift the ring up to the light of the window, and study it, turning it round slowly as if it were a diamond.

Finally, what Cesare had been waiting for occurred; the train slowed down and stopped at a village station, not too large and not too small; the halt looked like being a short one, as the train remained on the main line in one section. Cesare got down, and began to walk up and down the platform. He held the ring half hidden against his chest, under his jacket. He approached the Russian peasants who were waiting, one by one, with a conspiratorial air, half showed it to them, and whispered nervously: '*Tovarishch, zèloto, zèloto!*' ('gold').

At first the Russians did not listen to him. Then an old man looked closely at the ring, and asked the price; Cesare, without hesitating, said: '*Sto*' ('one hundred'); a modest enough price for a gold ring, a criminal one for a brass ring. The old man offered forty. Cesare pretended to be indignant and turned to somebody else. He continued like this with various clients, protracting matters and looking for the person who offered most; meantime, he kept an ear open for the engine whistle, in order to conclude the business and jump on to the train as it was leaving.

While Cesare was showing the ring to various people, we could see others discussing in small groups, suspicious and excited. At that moment the engine whistled; Cesare yielded the ring to the last bidder, pocketed about fifty rubles, and rapidly climbed onto the train, which was already moving. The train ran for one, two, ten yards; then it slowed down again, and stopped with a great screeching of brakes.

Cesare had closed the running doors and was peering out of the gap, at first triumphant, then worried, finally terrified. The man with the ring was showing his acquisition to the other peasants; these passed it from hand to hand, turned it over on all sides, and shook their heads with an air of doubt and disapproval. Then we saw the incautious purchaser, evidently repentant, raise his head and march resolutely along the train, in search of Cesare's refuge; an easy search, as ours was the only truck with its doors closed.

The matter was taking a decidedly bad turn; the Russian, who was clearly no genius, perhaps would not have managed to identify the truck by himself, but two or three of his colleagues were already pointing with energy in the right direction. Cesare suddenly jumped back from his spy hole, and had recourse to an extreme measure; he crouched in a corner of the truck, and made us conceal him hastily under all the available coverings. In a short time he disappeared under an enormous mass of blankets, eiderdowns, sacks and jackets; from which, listening carefully, I seemed to hear, muted and faint, and blasphemous in that context, words of prayer emerge.

We could already hear the Russians shouting in front of the truck, and banging against the doors, when the train moved off again with a violent jerk. Cesare re-emerged, as white as death, but recovered immediately: 'Now let them look for me!'

The following morning, under a radiant sun, the train stopped at Kazàtin. The name did not seem new to me; where had I read or heard it? Perhaps in war bulletins? But I had the impression of a nearer, more immediate recollection, as if someone had spoken to me about it at length recently;

after, and not before, the Auschwitz caesura, which snapped in two the chain of my memories.

Suddenly, standing on the platform, immediately in front of our truck, I saw my nebulous recollection personified: Galina, the girl from Katowice, the translator-dancer-typist of the Kommandantur, Galina of Kazàtin. I got down to greet her, full of joy and amazement at so improbable a meeting: to find my only Russian friend in this boundless land!

She had not changed very much; she was a little better dressed, and sheltered from the sun under a pretentious parasol. Nor had I changed much, at least externally; a little less puny and under-nourished than before, though just as ragged; but rich with a new wealth, the train standing behind me, the slow but sure engine, Italy nearer every day. She wished me a happy return; we exchanged a few hurried and embarrassed words, in a language which was neither hers nor mine, in the cold language of the invader, and we separated immediately, as the train was leaving. In the truck, which was jolting towards the frontier, I sat and smelt the cheap perfume which her hand had left on mine, happy that I had seen her again, sad at the memory of the hours spent in her company, of things unsaid, of opportunities unseized.

We passed through Zhmerinka once more, with suspicion, remembering the days of anguish we had spent there a few months before; but the train proceeded without difficulties, and on the evening of 19th September, after crossing Bessarabia rapidly, we were on the Pruth, at the border. In the deep gloom, as a sort of dismal farewell, the Soviet frontier police carried out a tumultuous and disorderly inspection of the train, searching (so they told us) for rubles, which it was forbidden to export; not that it mattered, as we had spent them all. We crossed the bridge, and slept on the other side, in the stationary train, anxious for the light of day to reveal Rumanian soil to us.

It was in fact a dramatic sight. When we threw open the doors in the early morning, a surprisingly domestic scene opened out before our eyes; no longer a deserted, geological steppe, but the green hills of Moldavia, with farms, haystacks and rows of vines; no longer enigmatic Cyrillic signs, but, right in front of our truck, a decrepit hovel, blue-green with verdigris, with clear writing on it, curiously similar to the Italian words: '*Paine, Lapte, Vin, Carnaciuri de Purcel*', bread, milk, wine, pork sausages. And in fact, in front of the hovel there was a woman, who was pulling an enormously long sausage out of a basket at her feet, and measuring it by lengths like string.

We saw peasants like our own, with broiled faces and pale foreheads, dressed in black, with jackets and waistcoats and watch-chains over their bellies; girls on foot or on bicycles, dressed almost like ours, whom we could have mistaken for Venetian or Abruzzese peasant girls. There were goats, sheep, cows, pigs, chickens. But, standing at a railway crossing, to act as a check to any precocious illusion of home, was a camel, driving us back into another world; a worn-out, grey, woolly camel, laden with sacks, exhaling haughtiness and stupid solemnity from his prehistoric leporine muzzle. The language of the place sounded equally mixed to our ears; well-known roots and terminations, but entangled and contaminated in a millenary common growth, could be heard alongside others, of a strange wild sound; a speech familiar in its music, hermetic in its sense.

At the frontier took place the complicated and difficult ceremony of transference from the ramshackle trucks of Soviet-gauge lines to others, equally ramshackle, with a western gauge; and soon after we entered the station of Iasi, where the train was laboriously broken up into three parts; a sign that the halt would last for many hours.

At Iasi two notable things occurred; the two German women from the woods appeared from nowhere, and all the married 'Rumanians' disappeared. The smuggling of the two Germans across the Soviet border must have been organized with great audacity and ability by a group of Italian soldiers; we never learnt the exact details, but rumour had it that the two girls had spent the critical night of the passage across the frontier hidden under the floor of the truck, secreted between the rods and the suspension. We saw them walking on the platform the next morning, offhand and arrogant, bundled up in Soviet military clothes and covered in mud and grease. Now they felt safe.

Simultaneously, we saw violent family conflicts explode in the trucks of the 'Rumanians'. Many of them, who had formerly belonged to the diplomatic corps or had been demobilized or had demobilized themselves from the ARMIR, had settled in Rumania and had married Rumanian women. At the end of the war, almost all of them had opted for repatriation, and the Russians had organized a train for them which should have taken them to Odessa, to embark there; but at Zhmerinka they had been attached to our luckless train, and had followed our fate; we never knew if this had happened through design or negligence. The Rumanian wives were furious with their Italian husbands; they had had enough of surprises and adventures and journeys and encampments. Now they had re-entered Rumanian territory, they were at home, they wanted to stay there and they would not listen to reason; some argued and wept, others tried to drag their husbands on to the platform, the wildest hurled their luggage and household possessions out of the trucks, while their children, terrified, ran screaming all around. The Russians of the escort had run to the scene, but they understood nothing and stood and looked on, inert and undecided.

As the halt at Iasi threatened to last all day, we left the station and wandered through the deserted streets, between low mud-coloured houses. A single, minute, archaic tram ran from one end of the city to the other; the ticket collector stood at a terminal; he spoke Yiddish, he was a Jew. With some effort we managed to understand each other. He informed me that other trainloads of ex-prisoners had passed through Iasi, of all races, French, English, Greek, Italian, Dutch, American. In many of these there had been Jews in need of assistance; so the local Jewish community had formed a relief centre. If we had one or two hours to spare, he counselled us to go as a delegation to the centre; we should be given advice and help. In fact, as his tram was about to leave, he told us to climb on, he would put us down at the right stop and would take care of the tickets.

Leonardo, Mr Unverdorben and I went; we crossed the dead city and reached a squalid, crumbling building, with temporary boarding in place of the doors and windows. Two old patriarchs, with a scarcely more opulent or flourishing air than ours, received us in a gloomy, dusty office; but they were full of affectionate kindness and good intentions, they made us sit on the only three chairs, overwhelmed us with attention and precipitately recounted to us, in Yiddish and French, the terrible trials which they and a few others had survived. They were prone to tears and laughter; at the moment of departure, they invited us peremptorily to drink a toast with terrible rectified alcohol, and gave us a basket of grapes to distribute among the Jews on the train. They also emptied all the drawers and their own pockets, and raked together a sum of *lei* which on the spot seemed to us astronomical; but, later, after we had divided it, and taken into account the inflation, we realized that its value was principally symbolic.

16. From Iasi to the Line

FOR SEVERAL DAYS we continued to travel towards the south, by small stages, across a countryside still enjoying summer, past towns and villages with barbaric, resounding names (Ciurea, Scantea, Vaslui, Piscu, Bràila, Pogoanele); on the night of 23rd September we saw the fires of the petroleum wells of Ploesti blazing; then our mysterious pilot turned west, and the following day we realized from the position of the sun that our course had been inverted; we were once more navigating towards the north. Without recognizing them, we admired the castles of Sinaia, a royal residence.

By now our truckload had exhausted all its ready money, and had sold or exchanged everything, however small, which was thought to possess commercial value. Consequently, apart from occasional strokes of luck or lawless exploits, our only source of food was what the Russians gave us; the situation was not dramatic, but confused and enervating.

It never became clear who was responsible for the victualling; most probably the Russians of the escort, who drew at random the most ill-assorted, or perhaps the only available, rations from every military or civilian depot within reach. Whenever the train stopped and was uncoupled, each truck sent two delegates to the Russians' truck, which was slowly transformed into a chaotic travelling bazaar; the Russians, with no regard for rules, distributed to these delegates provisions for their respective trucks. It was a daily game of chance; as regards quantity, the rations were sometimes scarce, sometimes Gargantuan, sometimes non-existent; and as regards quality, as unforeseeable as all things Russian. We received carrots, and yet more carrots, and yet still more carrots, for days on end; then the carrots disappeared, and the beans arrived. They were dry beans, as hard as pebbles; to cook them, we had to soak them for hours in whatever vessel we could lay our hands on, bowls, tins, pots, which we then hung from the roof of the truck; at night, when the train braked abruptly, this hanging forest oscillated violently, water and beans poured down on the sleepers, and scuffles, mirth and upheavals resulted in the dark. Potatoes came, then *kasha*, then gherkins, but without oil; then oil, half a bowl a person, when the gherkins were finished; then sunflower seeds, an exercise in patience. One day we received bread and sausage in abundance, and everybody breathed again; then grain for a week on end, as if we were chickens.

Only the family-trucks had stoves on board; the rest of us managed to cook on the ground on camp fires which we lit in haste as soon as the train stopped, and put out half-way through the cooking, amid quarrels and oaths, when the train set off again. We cooked intensely, furiously, listening for the whistle of the engine, with one eye on the starving vagrants, who emerged at once in crowds from the countryside, attracted by the smoke, like bloodhounds by a scent. We cooked like our forefathers, on three stones; and as stones could not always be found, every truck ended by possessing its own. Spits and ingenious devices appeared; Cantarella's pots re-emerged.

The problem of wood and water became urgent and compelling. Necessity simplifies: private woodpiles were raided in a flash; snow barriers, which in those countries were piled up alongside the rail tracks in the summer months, were stolen; fences, railway sleepers, once (for want of anything better) an entire goods truck abandoned after an accident, were demolished; in our truck the presence of the Moor and his famous axe was providential. As for water, in the first place we needed suitable vessels, which meant that every truck had to procure a bucket, by barter, theft or purchase. Our bucket, legitimately bought, revealed a leak at the first experiment; we repaired it with a piece of plaster from the surgery, and it miraculously withstood the cooking as far as the Brenner, when it peeled off.

Normally it was impossible to collect a supply of water at the stations; an endless queue formed in front of the fountain (when there was one) in a few seconds, and only a few buckets could be filled. Some people crept stealthily to the tender which held the water for the engine; but if the driver saw them, he would fly into a rage, and bombard these rash persons with oaths and burning coal. Nevertheless, we sometimes managed to tap hot water from the belly of the engine itself; it was slimy, rusty water, unsuitable for cooking but quite useful for washing.

The best sources were country wells. The train often stopped in the fields, at a red signal; it was impossible to foresee whether the halt would last a few seconds or hours. So we all hastily unbuckled our trouser belts to knot together and form a long rope; then the nimblest person in the truck rushed off, with the rope and bucket, in search of a well. I was the nimblest person in my truck, and I often succeeded in the enterprise; but once I ran a serious risk of losing the train. I had already dropped the bucket into the well and was lifting it laboriously, when I heard the engine whistle. If I lost the bucket and belts, our precious common property, I should dishonour myself for ever; so I pulled up the bucket with all my strength, got hold of it, poured the water on the ground, and ran off, hampered by the knotted belts, towards the train, which was already moving. A second's delay could mean a month's delay; I ran without stopping, for my life, jumped over two hedges and the fence, and rushed over the slippery gravel of the rail-bed as the train slid past me. My truck had already gone by; charitable hands from other trucks stretched out towards me, gripped the belts and the bucket, while yet more hands grabbed my hair, shoulders, clothing, and hoisted me onto the floor of the last truck, where I lay semi-conscious for a long time.

The train continued to move north; it entered an increasingly narrow valley, crossed the Transylvanian Alps through the Predeal Pass on 24th September, amid austere naked mountains, in bitter cold, and descended on Brasov. Here the engine was detached, guarantee of a long halt, and the customary ceremonial began to take place; people with a furtive ferocious air, with hatchets in their hands, wandered round the station and outside; others with buckets quarrelled over the little water; others still stole hay from the haystacks, or transacted business with the local inhabitants; children wandered around in search of trouble or small opportunities to steal; women washed clothing or themselves in public, exchanged visits and passed on news from truck to truck, rekindled ill-digested quarrels, and sparked off new ones. The fires were immediately lit, and we began to cook.

Next to our train stood a Soviet military convoy, full of lorries, armoured cars and fuel tankers. It was guarded by two robust female soldiers, in boots and helmets, with guns on their shoulders, and fixed bayonets; they were of indefinable age and of gnarled, unprepossessing appearance. When they saw fires being lit just in front of the petrol tankers, they grew rightly indignant at our irresponsibility and, shouting 'nelzya nelzya', ordered them to be put out immediately.

Everybody obeyed, cursing; everybody, except a handful from the Alpine Brigade, hardboiled types, veterans of the Russian campaign, who had rustled up a goose and were roasting it. They held council with sober words, while the two women fulminated at their backs; then two of them, nominated by the majority, got up, with the severe and resolute faces of men about to sacrifice themselves conscientiously for the common good. They advanced on the women soldiers face to face and spoke to them in a low voice. The negotiations were surprisingly short; the women put down their helmets and arms, then the four, serious and composed, left the station, took a narrow path and disappeared from our view. They returned a quarter of an hour later, the women in front, a little less gnarled and with slightly congested faces, the men behind, dignified and calm. The goose was nearly ready; the four squatted on the ground with the others, the goose was carved up and divided in pieces, then, after the brief truce, the Russian women resumed their weapons and their duties.

From Brasov our route once more turned to the west, towards the Hungarian frontier. Rain began to fall steadily and worsened the situation; it was difficult to light the fires, we were wearing our only set of clothing, mud soaked in everywhere. The roof of our truck was not watertight; only a few square yards of the floor remained inhabitable, as water dripped down pitilessly on the rest. Quarrels and disputes broke out endlessly when it was time to go to bed.

It is an age-old observation that in every human group there is a predestined victim; one who inspires contempt, whom all mock, about whom stupid malignant gossip grows, on whom, by some mysterious agreement, all unload their bad tempers and their desire to hurt. The victim of our truck was the Carabiniere. It would be difficult to establish the reason why, if a reason existed; the Carabiniere was a young Abruzzese, polite, mild, helpful, with a pleasant appearance. He was not even particularly obtuse, in fact he was rather touchy and sensitive, and consequently suffered acutely from the persecution to which he was subjected by the other soldiers in the truck. But there it was, he was a Carabiniere; and it is well known that there is little love lost between the Force (so called by antonomasia) and the other armed forces. Carabinieri are reproved, perversely, for their excessive discipline, seriousness, chastity, honesty, their lack of humour, their indiscriminate obedience, their habits, their uniform. Fantastic, grotesque, inept legends circulate about them, and are handed down in barracks from generation to generation: the legend of the hammer, the legend of the oath. I shall say nothing of the first, which is too infamous; as regards the latter, the version I heard was that the young recruit to the Force is obliged to swear a secret, loathsome, infernal oath, in which, among other things, he solemnly pledges 'to kill his father and mother'; and that every Cara-biniere either has killed them or will kill them, otherwise he will fail to win promotion. Our poor little wretch could not even open his mouth: 'You keep quiet, you who've killed father and mother.' But he never rebelled; he accepted this and a hundred other insults with the adamantine patience of a saint. One day he took me aside, as a neutral observer, and assured me 'that the business of the oath was not true.'

For three days, virtually without stopping, we travelled in the rain, which made us bad-tempered and mean, only halt-ing once for a few hours at a village full of mud, with the glorious name of Alba Julia. On the evening of 26th Septem-ber, after travelling more than five hundred miles on Ruman-ian soil, we reached the Hungarian frontier, near Arad, at a village called Curtici.

I am convinced that the inhabitants of Curtici still remem-ber the scourge of our passage; in all probability it has now become one of the local legends, and will be talked of round the fire for generations, as elsewhere they will still speak of Attila and Tamburlane. This detail of our journey is also destined to remain obscure; according to all the evidence, the Rumanian military or railway authorities no longer wanted us or had already 'off-loaded' us, while the Hun-garian authorities did not want to accept us, or had not 'taken over the consignment'; as a result, we remained riveted to Curtici, we and the train and the escort, for seven exhausting days, and we devastated the place.

Curtici was an agricultural village with perhaps a thousand inhabitants, and possessed very little; we were fourteen hundred, and had need of everything. In the seven days we emptied all the wells, exhausted the supplies of wood, and caused grave damage to everything in the station that could be burnt; as for the station latrines, it is better not to speak of them. We provoked a fearful increase in the price of milk, bread, maize, poultry; after which, once our purchasing power had been reduced to zero, thefts occurred by night, and later also by day. Geese, which as far as we could see constituted the main local wealth, and initially circulated freely along the muddy paths in solemn well-ordered flotillas, disappeared completely, partly captured, partly shut up in their coops.

Every morning we opened our doors with the absurd hope that the train might have moved without our realizing, while we were asleep; but nothing had changed, the sky was always black and rainy, the muddy houses always facing us, the train as inert and impotent as a stranded ship. We bent down to examine the wheels, those wheels which were supposed to take us home; but no, they had not moved an inch, they seemed soldered to the tracks, and the rain was turning them rusty. We were cold and hungry, and we felt abandoned and forgotten.

On the sixth day, enervated and envenomed more than the rest of us, Cesare abandoned us. He declared that he had had enough of Curtici, of the Russians, of the train and of us; that he did not want to go mad, or to die of hunger, or be cut to pieces by the locals; that when a man was on his toes he got along better by himself. He added that, if we wanted, we could always follow him; but his terms were clear: he was fed up with living in want, he was ready to take risks, but he wanted to cut it short, make money rapidly, and return to Rome by plane. None of us felt up to following him, and Cesare left; he took a train for Bucharest, had many adventures, and succeeded in his intention, that is, he returned to Rome by air, although later than us; but that is another story, a story *'de haulte graisse'*, which I shall not recount, or shall recount elsewhere, only if and when Cesare gives me permission.

If in Rumania I had enjoyed a delicate philological pleasure at such names as Galati, Alba Julia, Turnu Severin, immediately we entered Hungary I was confronted with Békéscsaba, followed by Hódmezövasárhely and Kiskunfélegyháza. The Hungarian plain had turned into a marsh, the sky was a leaden colour, but we were saddened above all by Cesare's absence. He had left a painful emptiness among us; in his absence, nobody knew what to speak of, nobody managed any longer to conquer the boredom of the interminable journey, the fatigue of the nineteen days of rail-travel which weighed upon us. We looked at each other with a vague sense of guilt; why had we allowed him to leave? But in Hungary, despite the impossible names, we now felt ourselves in Europe, protected by a civilization which was ours, sheltered from alarming apparitions such as that of the camel in Moldavia. The train moved towards Budapest, but did not enter it; on 6th October it stopped more than once at Ujpest and other suburban stations, leaving us with ghostly visions of ruins, temporary huts and deserted roads; then it moved into the plain once more, in gusts of rain and a film of autumn mist.

It stopped at Szób on market day; we all got down to stretch our legs and spend the little money we possessed. I no longer had anything; but I was hungry, and bartered my Auschwitz jacket, which I had jealously preserved until then, for a noble mixture of fermented cheese and onions, whose acute aroma had conquered me. When the engine whistled, and we climbed into the truck, we counted ourselves and found that we were two more than before.

One was Vincenzo, and no-one was surprised. Vincenzo

was a difficult boy; a Calabrian shepherd of sixteen, who had somehow ended up in Germany. He was as wild as the Velletrano, but of different temperament: as timid, reserved and contemplative as the latter was violent and bloodthirsty. He had wonderful blue eyes, almost feminine, and a fine, expressive, dreamy face; he hardly ever spoke. He was a nomad at heart, restless, attracted by the woods at Starye Dorogi as if by invisible demons; on the train, too, he had no stable residence in any one truck, but wandered through all of them. We understood the reason for his instability immediately; no sooner had the train left Szób than Vincenzo collapsed to the ground with the whites of his eyes showing and his jaws clenched like a vice. He roared like a beast, and fought, stronger than the four soldiers who held him down: an epileptic fit. He had certainly had others, at Starye Dorogi and before; but every time he had felt the warning signs, urged on by his fierce pride, he had taken refuge in the forest, so that no-one should know of his illness; or, perhaps, he fled in the face of the illness, like birds before a storm. During the long journey, as he could not stay on the ground, he changed truck when he felt the attack approaching. He stayed with us only a few days, then he disappeared; we found him roosting on the roof of another truck. Why? He replied that he could see the countryside better up there.

The other new guest, for different reasons, also presented a difficult case. Nobody knew him; he was a robust youth, barefoot, dressed in a Red Army jacket and trousers. He spoke only Hungarian and none of us were able to understand him. The Carabiniere told us that the boy had approached him while he was eating some bread at the village, and had stretched out his hand; he had given him half his food, and from then on had not managed to shake him off; the boy must have followed him without anyone noticing, while we were all climbing hurriedly into the truck.

He was well received; one mouth more to feed was not a worry. He was an intelligent, cheerful boy; as soon as the train started, he introduced himself with great dignity. His name was Pista and he was fourteen. Father and mother? Here it was more difficult to understand each other; I found a pencil stub and a piece of paper, and drew a man, a woman and a child between them; I pointed to the child and said 'Pista'; then I waited. Pista turned grave, and then sketched a drawing which was all too painfully obvious: a house, an aeroplane, a falling bomb. Then he cancelled the house, and drew a large smoking heap beside it. But he was not in a mood for sad things; he screwed up the sheet, asked for another, and drew a cask, with remarkable precision: the bottom and all the visible staves in the right perspective; then the hoops, and the hole with the tap. We looked at each other puzzled; what did the message mean? Pista laughed happily; then he drew himself next to it, with a hammer in one hand and a saw in the other. Hadn't we understood yet? This was his trade, he was a cooper.

Everybody liked him immediately; moreover, he tried to be useful; he swept the floor every morning, enthusiastically washed the bowls, went to fetch water, and was happy when we sent him 'shopping' to his compatriots at the various halts. He could already make himself understood in Italian by the time we reached the Brenner; he sang beautiful songs of his country, which no-one understood, and then sought to explain them with gestures, making us all laugh whole-heartedly, himself first of all. He was as fond of the Carabiniere as a younger brother, and slowly cleansed him of his original sin: true, the Carabiniere had killed his father and mother, but, all told, he must be a good boy, since Pista followed him. He filled up the gap left by Cesare. We asked him why he had come with us, what brought him to Italy; but we were unable to understand, partly because of the difficulty of conversing, but above all because he himself did not know. He had wandered round stations like a stray dog for months; he had followed the first human creature who had looked at him with pity.

We had hoped to cross from Hungary into Austria without further frontier complications, but it was not so easy; on the morning of 7th October, the twenty-second day of our journey, we reached Bratislava in Slovakia, in sight of the Beskidy, the same mountains which had closed the lugubrious horizon of Auschwitz. Another language, another coinage, another route; would we now complete the circle? Katowice was 120 miles away; would we begin another vain, exhausting circuit of Europe? But we entered German territory in the evening; on the 8th we were stranded at the goods depot of Leopoldau, a suburban station of Vienna, and we felt almost at home.

The suburbs of Vienna were ugly and casual like those we knew at Milan and Turin and, like the last visions we recalled of those cities, were reduced to rubble by bombardment. Passers-by were few: women, children, old people, not a single man. Paradoxically, their language also sounded familiar to me; some even understood Italian. We changed what money we possessed at random for local money, but it was useless; as at Cracow in March, all the shops were closed, or sold only rationed goods. 'But what can one buy at Vienna without a ration card?' I asked a little girl no more than twelve years old. She was dressed in rags, but wore shoes with high heels and was heavily made up: '*Überhaupt nichts,*' she replied contemptuously.

We returned to the train to sleep; during the night we travelled a few miles, with much jolting and screeching, and found ourselves transferred to another station, Vienna-Jedlersdorf. Next to us another train emerged from the fog, or rather the corpse of a train: the engine was standing on end, absurdly, its muzzle pointing to the sky as if it meant to climb there; all the trucks were charred. We approached, driven by an instinct for plunder and by a curiosity tinged with mockery; we promised ourselves a malignant satisfaction in laying hands on the ruins of these German objects. But derision was answered by derision: one truck contained odd scraps of metal which must have belonged to musical instruments that had been burnt, and hundreds of earthenware ocarinas, the only things to survive; another truck was full of regulation pistols, melted and rusted; the third held a tangle of curved sabres, which the fire and rain had soldered into their scabbards for all eternity: vanity of vanities, and the cold taste of perdition.

We walked away, and wandered round until we found ourselves on the banks of the Danube. The river was in flood, turbid, yellow and threateningly swollen; at that point its course is almost straight, and we could see, one behind the other, in a misty nightmare perspective, seven bridges, all smashed exactly at the centre, all with their broken segments plunging into the eddying water. As we returned to our itinerant dwelling, we were startled by the clanging noise of a tram, the sole sign of life. It was running crazily on the loose rails, along the deserted avenues, without halting at the stops. We saw the driver at his post, as pale as a ghost; behind him, delirious with enthusiasm, stood the seven Russians of our escort, and not another passenger: it was the first tram they had ever travelled in. Some hung out of the windows and cheered, while others incited and threatened the driver into increasing his speed.

There was a market on a big square; once again a spontaneous and illegal market, but far more wretched and furtive than the Polish ones I had frequented with the Greek and Cesare; in fact, it reminded me strongly of another scene, the Exchange at the Lager, indelible in our memories. There were no stalls, but people on their feet, shivering and restless, in little cliques, ready to run away, with their bags and suitcases in their hands and their pockets swollen; they exchanged minute trifles, potatoes, slices of bread, loose cigarettes, small items of worn-out rubbish from their homes.

We climbed into our trucks with heavy hearts. We had felt no joy in seeing Vienna undone and the Germans broken, but rather anguish: not compassion, but a larger anguish, which was mixed up with our own misery, with the heavy, threatening sensation of an irreparable and definitive evil which was present everywhere, nestling like gangrene in the guts of Europe and the world, the seed of future harm.

The train seemed unable to tear itself away from Vienna; after three days of halts and manoeuvres, on 10th October, hungry, drenched and wretched, we found ourselves at Nussdorf, another suburb. But on the morning of the 11th, as if it had suddenly picked up a lost scent, the train moved decisively towards the west; with unaccustomed speed it passed through St Polten, Loosdorf and Amstetten, and in the evening a sign appeared on the road which ran parallel to the railway, as portentous to our eyes as the birds which tell navigators of land nearby. It was a vehicle unknown to us: a squat, graceless, military vehicle, as flat as a tin can with a white, and not a red, star painted on its side: in short, a jeep. A Negro was driving it; one of the occupants waved his arms at us, and shouted in Neapolitan dialect: 'You're going home, you bums!'

Clearly the demarcation line was nearby; we reached it at St Valentin, a few miles from Linz. Here we had to get down; we said good-bye to the young barbarians of the escort and to our excellent engine-driver, and passed into American hands.

Almost by definition, it can be said of transit camps that the shorter the average stay, the worse the organization. At St Valentin one stopped only for a few hours, a day at the most, and consequently it was an extremely dirty and primitive camp. There was no lighting, no heating, no beds: we slept on the bare wooden floor, in frightfully decrepit huts, in the middle of ankle-deep mud. The only efficient equipment was in the baths and the disinfection room; the West took possession of us by this form of purification and exorcism.

A few gigantic, taciturn G.I.s, unarmed, but embellished with a myriad of gadgets whose significance and use escaped us, were responsible for this ritual task. Everything went well with the bath; there were about twenty wooden cabins, with lukewarm showers and bath wraps, a luxury never seen again. After the bath, they took us to a vast brick room, divided in two by a cable on which ten curious implements were hanging, vaguely similar to pneumatic drills; we could hear an air compressor pulsating outside. All fourteen hundred, that is all of us, were crammed to one side of the division, men and women together; and at this point ten officials appeared on the scene, with a science-fiction attire, wrapped up in white overalls, with helmets and gas masks. They seized the first of the flock, and without wasting time stuck the tubes of the hanging instruments into all the openings of their clothes in turn: under collars and belts, into pockets, up trouser legs, under skirts. They were a sort of pneumatic blower, which blew out insecticide: the insecticide was DDT, an absolute novelty to us, like the jeeps, penicillin and the atomic bomb, which we learnt about soon afterwards.

Everybody accommodated himself to the treatment, swearing or laughing from the tickling, until it came to the turn of a naval officer and his beautiful fiancée. When the hooded men laid chaste but rough hands on her, the officer placed himself decisively in between. He was a robust and resolute young man: woe betide anyone who touched his woman.

The perfect mechanism stopped abruptly; the hoods consulted briefly, with inarticulate nasal sounds, then one of them took off his mask and overalls and planted himself in front of the officer with his fists at the ready for a fight. The others formed an orderly circle, and a regular boxing match began. After a few minutes of silent and gentlemanly combat, the officer fell to the ground with a bleeding nose; the girl, shaken and pale, was dusted all over according to the regulations, but without anger or vengefulness and everything re-established itself in American order.

17. The Awakening

AUSTRIA BORDERS ON Italy, and St Valentin is only 180 miles from Tarvisio; but on 15th October, the thirty-first day of our journey, we crossed a new frontier and entered Munich, prey to a disconsolate railway tiredness, a permanent loathing for trains, for snatches of sleep on wooden floors, for jolting and for stations; so that familiar smells, common to all the railways of the world, the sharp smell of impregnated sleepers, hot brakes, burning fuel, inspired in us a deep disgust. We were tired of everything, tired in particular of perforating useless frontiers.

But from another point of view, the fact of feeling a piece of Germany under our feet for the first time, not a piece of Upper Silesia or of Austria, but of Germany itself, overlaid our tiredness with a complex attitude composed of intolerance, frustration and tension. We felt we had something to say, enormous things to say, to every single German, and we felt that every German should have something to say to us; we felt an urgent need to settle our accounts, to ask, explain and comment, like chess players at the end of a game. Did 'they' know about Auschwitz, about the silent daily massacre, a step away from their doors? If they did, how could they walk about, return home and look at their children, cross the threshold of a church? If they did not, they ought, as a sacred duty, to listen, to learn everything, immediately, from us, from me; I felt the tattooed number on my arm burning like a sore.

As I wandered around the streets of Munich, full of ruins, near the station where our train lay stranded once more, I felt I was moving among throngs of insolvent debtors, as if everybody owed me something, and refused to pay. I was among them, in the enemy camp, among the *Herrenvolk*; but the men were few, many were mutilated, many dressed in rags like us. I felt that everybody should interrogate us, read in our faces who we were, and listen to our tale in humility. But no-one looked us in the eyes, no-one accepted the challenge; they were deaf, blind and dumb imprisoned in their ruins, as in a fortress of wilful ignorance, still strong, still capable of hatred and contempt, still prisoners of their old tangle of pride and guilt.

I found myself searching among them, among that anonymous crowd of sealed faces, for other faces, clearly stamped in my memory, many bearing a name: the name of someone who could not but know, remember, reply; who had commanded and obeyed, killed, humiliated, corrupted. A vain and foolish search; because not they, but others, the few just ones, would reply for them.

If we had taken one guest on board at Szób, after Munich we realized that we had taken on board an entire contingent: our train consisted no longer of sixty, but of sixty-one trucks. A new truck was travelling with us towards Italy at the end of our train, crammed with young Jews, boys and girls, coming from all the countries of Eastern Europe. None of them seemed more than twenty years old, but they were extremely self-confident and resolute people; they were young Zionists, on their way to Israel, travelling where they were able to, and finding a path where they could. A ship was waiting for them at Bari; they had purchased their truck, and it had proved the simplest thing in the world to attach it to our train: they had not asked anybody's permission, but had hooked it on, and that was that. I was amazed, but they laughed at my amazement: 'Hitler's dead, isn't he?' replied their leader, with his intense hawk-like glance. They felt immensely free and strong, lords of the world and of their destinies.

We passed through Garmisch-Partenkirchen and in the evening reached the fantastically disordered transit camp of Mittenwald, in the mountains, on the Austrian border. We spent the night there, and it was our last night of cold. The following day the train ran down to Innsbruck, where it filled up with Italian smugglers, who brought us the greetings of our homeland, in the absence of official authorities, and generously distributed chocolate, grappa and tobacco.

As the train, more tired than us, climbed towards the Italian frontier it snapped in two like an overtaut cable; there were several injuries, but this was the last adventure. Late at night we crossed the Brenner, which we had passed in our exile twenty months before; our less tired companions celebrated with a cheerful uproar; Leonardo and I remained lost in a silence crowded with memories. Of 650, our number when we had left, three of us were returning. And how much had we lost, in those twenty months? What should we find at home? How much of ourselves had been eroded, extinguished? Were we returning richer or poorer, stronger or emptier? We did not know; but we knew that on the thresholds of our homes, for good or ill, a trial awaited us, and we anticipated it with fear. We felt in our veins the poison of Auschwitz, flowing together with our thin blood; where should we find the strength to begin our lives again, to break down the barriers, the brushwood which grows up spontaneously in all absences, around every deserted house, every empty refuge? Soon, tomorrow, we should have to give battle, against enemies still unknown, outside ourselves and inside; with what weapons, what energies, what willpower? We felt the weight of centuries on our shoulders, we felt oppressed by a year of ferocious memories; we felt emptied and defenceless. The months just past, although hard, of wandering on the margins of civilization now seemed to us like a truce, a parenthesis of unlimited availability, a providential but unrepeatable gift of fate.

With these thoughts, which kept us from sleep, we passed our first night in Italy, as the train slowly descended the deserted, dark Adige Valley. On 17th October, we reached the camp of Pescantina, near Verona, and here we split up, everyone following his own destiny; but no train left in the direction of Turin until the evening of the following day. In the confused vortex of thousands of refugees and displaced persons, we glimpsed Pista, who had already found his path; he wore the white and yellow armband of the Pontifical Organization of Assistance, and collaborated briskly and cheerfully in the life of the camp. And then we saw advance towards us a figure, a well-known face, a full head higher than the crowd, the Moor of Verona. He had come to say good-bye to us, to Leonardo and me; he had reached his home, the first of all of us, for Avesa, his village, was only a few miles away. And he blessed us, the old blasphemer: he raised two enormous knobbly fingers, and blessed us with the solemn gesture of a Pontiff, wishing us a good return and a happy future.

I reached Turin on 19th October, after thirty-five days of travel; my house was still standing, all my family was alive, no-one was expecting me. I was swollen, bearded and in rags, and had difficulty in making myself recognized. I found my friends full of life, the warmth of secure meals, the solidity of daily work, the liberating joy of recounting my story. I found a large clean bed, which in the evening (a moment of terror) yielded softly under my weight. But only after many months did I lose the habit of walking with my glance fixed to the ground, as if searching for something to eat or to pocket hastily or to sell for bread; and a dream full of horror has still not ceased to visit me, at sometimes frequent, sometimes longer, intervals.

It is a dream within a dream, varied in detail, one in substance. I am sitting at a table with my family, or with friends,

221

or at work, or in the green countryside; in short, in a peaceful relaxed environment, apparently without tension or affliction; yet I feel a deep and subtle anguish, the definite sensation of an impending threat. And in fact, as the dream proceeds, slowly or brutally, each time in a different way, everything collapses and disintegrates around me, the scenery, the walls, the people, while the anguish becomes more intense and more precise. Now everything has changed to chaos; I am alone in the centre of a grey and turbid nothing, and now, I *know* what this thing means, and I also know that I have always known it; I am in the Lager once more, and nothing is true outside the Lager. All the rest was a brief pause, a deception of the senses, a dream; my family, nature in flower, my home. Now this inner dream, this dream of peace, is over, and in the outer dream, which continues, gelid, a well-known voice resounds: a single word, not imperious, but brief and subdued. It is the dawn command of Auschwitz, a foreign word, feared and expected: get up, '*Wstawàch*'.

Turin, December 1961–November 1962.